AF869603

PERSONAL FINANCE FOR TEENS SIMPLIFIED: INDEPENDENCE THROUGH FEARLESS WEALTH BUILDING

MASTER MONEY MANAGEMENT, SAVING, BUDGETING, INVESTMENTS, AND BANKING BASICS

JILLIAN D. QUINN

© Copyright 2023 - All rights reserved.

The content contained within this book may not be reproduced, duplicated or transmitted without direct written permission from the author or the publisher.

Under no circumstances will any blame or legal responsibility be held against the publisher, or author, for any damages, reparation, or monetary loss due to the information contained within this book, either directly or indirectly.

Legal Notice:

This book is copyright protected. It is only for personal use. You cannot amend, distribute, sell, use, quote or paraphrase any part, or the content within this book, without the consent of the author or publisher.

Disclaimer Notice:

Please note the information contained within this document is for educational and entertainment purposes only. All effort has been executed to present accurate, up to date, reliable, complete information. No warranties of any kind are declared or implied. Readers acknowledge that the author is not engaged in the rendering of legal, financial, medical or professional advice. The content within this book has been derived from various sources. Please consult a licensed professional before attempting any techniques outlined in this book.

By reading this document, the reader agrees that under no circumstances is the author responsible for any losses, direct or indirect, that are incurred as a result of the use of the information contained within this document, including, but not limited to, errors, omissions, or inaccuracies.

CONTENTS

Introduction 7

Part I
FINANCIAL FOUNDATIONS

1. THE FOUR PILLARS OF PERSONAL FINANCE 13
Assets and Liabilities: Your Financial See-Saw 15
Income and Expenses: The Money Dance 16
The Time Value of Money 17
Cool Ways to Develop the Right Money 'Tude 21
Examples of Compounding, Please! 24
Activity: Personal Finance Quiz 25

2. SETTING CLEAR AND MEANINGFUL GOALS 33
Brennan Puts a Sock in It 33
Why It's Totally Lit to Set Financial Goals: Nine Epic Benefits! 34
Leveling up Your Money Game: Short, Medium, and Long- Term Financial Goals 37
Step 1: The Power of SMART Goals 39
Step 2: Dream Big and Get Creative 41
Step 3: Make a Game Plan 42
Step 4: Keep the Momentum Going 43
Step 5: Share the Money Journey 44
Aligning Goals With Values 44
Set Your SMART Financial Goals 49
SMART Goal Templates 50

3. BUILDING A BUDGET FROM SCRATCH 53
Hart Main's Epic Journey: How a Teen Turned Teasing Into a Candle Empire 53
Budgeting Basics: How to Make Money Moves and Still Have Fun 54
Needs, Wants, and Moolah 58
Budgeting Apps 59
The 50/30/20 Budget 61

Delayed Gratification Leads to Financial Success 64
Activity: Budget Quiz 67

4. AN INTRODUCTION TO CHECKING ACCOUNTS 71
Alina's Lollipop Dream: From Tooth-Friendly Treats to Multi-Million Dollar Success 71
Why You Should Have a Bank Account 71
How to Open a Bank Account 73
Pros and Cons of Online Banking 80
Protect Your Bank Account From Fraudsters 83
Activity: Choosing the Right Bank for You 85

Part II
UNDERSTANDING SAVINGS AND INVESTMENTS

5. THE ART OF SAVING 89
You're Never Too Young to Start Saving 90
The Importance of an Emergency Fund 93
Unlocking the Moolah: How to Stack Your Cash 96
Types of Savings Accounts 100
Activity 104

6. COMPOUNDING WIZARDRY 107
Get a Head Start for Maximum Impact 108
Compound Growth on Investments and Interest 110
The Rule of 72 111
Activity 113

7. FUNDAMENTALS OF INVESTING 119
Fraser Doherty's SuperJam: A Teen's Sweet Success 119
Types of Investments: Stocks, Bonds, and More 120
Cryptocurrencies 124
Peer-to-Peer Lending 126
Risk and Reward: Understanding Investment Dynamics 129
Retirement Planning 134
Activity: Risk Tolerance Questionnaire 137

8. STARTING YOUR INVESTMENT JOURNEY 143
Dominic: The Teenage Scooter Millionaire 143
Investment Options for Teens and Young Adults 144
Exchange-traded funds (ETFs) 146

Fractional Share Investing 148
Index-Based ETFs 150
Robo-Advisors 152
Activity: What Is Your Investment Style? 156

Part III
NAVIGATING INCOME POTENTIAL

9. UNLEASHING YOUR ENTREPRENEURIAL SPIRIT 165
How to Start Your Business 166
The Benefits of Starting Your Own Business 169
Activity: Create a Business Plan 172

Part IV
DEMYSTIFYING DEBIT AND CREDIT

10. THE PITFALLS OF TOO MUCH DEBT 179
Understanding Good Debt Versus Bad Debt 180
Avoiding the Pitfalls of Too Much Debt 182
Activity: Quiz on Good Debt Versus Bad Debt 184

11. BUILDING A POSITIVE CREDIT HISTORY 191
Bella Tipping: Empowering Kids in Travel With Kidzcationz 191
The Importance of a Good Credit History 192
What Is a Credit Score? 195
Activity: Credit Score Quiz 198

Part V
STEPPING STONES TO SUCCESS: EDUCATION AND CAREER PATH

12. PLANNING YOUR CAREER AND HIGHER EDUCATION 205
What You Should Know 206
Navigating the World of College Finance: Financial Aid and Student Loans 210

Conclusion 217
References 223

INTRODUCTION

Imagine this: You're standing at the edge of a vast, uncharted wilderness. You've got a map in your hand, but you need help reading it. The terrain is filled with hidden traps and potential pitfalls, and you can't help but feel a little lost. You're not alone; many teens and young adults find themselves in a similar situation when it comes to personal finances.

According to recent statistics, 75% of teens need more confidence in their knowledge of personal finance. It's like wandering through that wilderness without a clear path, not knowing where to turn. In fact, 41% of teens don't even know what a 401(k) is, and 32% need help to distinguish between a credit card and a debit card. In 2021, 86% of teens expressed interest in investing, but a significant 45% refrained from investing because they lacked confidence (Turner, 2023).

But here's the catalyst that might have brought you to this book: the realization that you don't want to be a part of these statistics, that you want to be the exception. You understand that personal finance is a fundamental life skill, and you're determined not to be lost in the financial wilderness.

That's why you're holding this book. You're looking for answers, guidance, and a way to navigate the complex landscape of personal finances. This book is your map, compass, and guide through the financial wilderness. It's designed with one clear goal in mind: to provide you with the knowledge, tools, and confidence to secure your financial future.

Here's the good news: You won't have to navigate this financial wilderness blindfolded. This book presents the FUNDS framework, a roadmap that simplifies personal finance, making it accessible and understandable for teens and young adults like you. You'll discover the shortcuts to managing money, understanding investments, and building a solid financial foundation.

But don't just take my word for it. Let me share the inspiring story of Ollie Forsyth (Royale, 2020). Ollie's journey to success was far from conventional. Starting small, he sold friendship bracelets to his family and friends. Ollie, a teen with dyslexia, once believed he was a failure and endured the hardship of bullying. But he had an entrepreneurial spark that refused to dim.

At 12 years old, when most kids dream of their favorite video games, Ollie turned his bracelet- making hobby into a business. He began selling his colorful creations to friends and their parents. As demand grew, he took a bold step and launched Ollie's Shop, an online retailer, at 13. In the first few months, he made $5,000!

Ollie's passion didn't stop there. He woke up at 5 a.m. every day, juggling school and business, proving that age is just a number when it comes to achieving your dreams. But Ollie didn't stop at his own success. He founded The Budding Entrepreneur Club, a platform for young entrepreneurs to connect and share ideas.

Ollie Forsyth's story is a testament to the power of determination, proving that anyone can turn their passion into success, regardless of their challenges. So, don't let obstacles hold you back. If Ollie can do it, so can you!

By the time you finish this book, you'll be equipped with the knowledge and skills to take charge of your finances. You'll confidently navigate the world of banking, savings, investing, and budgeting. You'll make informed decisions that can lead to a life of financial security and freedom.

Gone are the days of financial stress and uncertainty. Instead, picture a life where you have the freedom to chase your dreams, where your financial goals are within reach, and where you're in control of your financial destiny.

Now, you might be wondering, "*Why should I trust the author of this book?*" The truth is, I've been in your shoes. I've faced the same financial challenges and uncertainties you're encountering now. I've made the mistakes and learned the lessons, so you don't have to.

I've worked tirelessly to gather the essential information, strategies, and tips you need to succeed on your financial journey. I'm here to be your mentor, sharing the knowledge and guidance I wish I'd had when I was starting.

As a parent of two teens myself and a financial advisor by profession, I understand the difficulties, the questions, and the fears that can come with managing money, and I'm committed to helping you overcome them. You've got the ambition, the drive, and the determination to master your finances, and I'm here to provide you with the roadmap to achieve it.

As you turn the page and embark on this journey, remember that you're not alone. There's a clear path ahead, and with the guidance you'll find in these pages, you'll be well-prepared to tackle the financial wilderness and emerge victorious.

So, whether you're a high school student, a college-bound teen, or a young adult, this book is your key to unlocking the mysteries of personal finance and taking control of your financial future. Let's venture together into the world of personal finances, armed with knowledge, confidence, and the determination to succeed.

PART I

FINANCIAL FOUNDATIONS

1

THE FOUR PILLARS OF PERSONAL FINANCE

Once upon a time, in a world of school lockers and teenage dreams, Maddie Bradshaw became the reigning queen of creativity (How to Become a Teenage Millionaire: 15 Success Stories, 2018).

It all started when Maddie, a 10-year-old with a vision, faced a common middle-school dilemma: Her boring locker needed some serious pizzazz!

Picture this: With determination, Maddie set out on a mission to make her locker the envy of every hallway. But there was a tiny hiccup; she couldn't find anything in the stores that matched her imagination. That's when fate (in the form of her uncle's non-operational coke machine) stepped in and gifted her a treasure trove of 50 bottle caps.

Maddie's genius kicked into high gear. She decided to transform those humble bottle caps into 50 tiny art pieces. But she didn't stop there! She added magnets to the back of these caps, turning them into magical decorations that would stick to the inside of her metal locker. The locker makeover blew away her friends, who also wanted a piece of the action.

But Maddie was just getting started. At the age of 12, armed with a few hundred dollars she'd been diligently putting away and the unwavering support of her amazing mother, who matched the amount she withdrew from her savings, she dreamed even bigger. Those bottle caps evolved into something extraordinary, 'Snap Caps!' These were no ordinary jewelry pieces but necklaces with interchangeable accessories and add-ons. They had a magnetic pendant, allowing the cap to latch onto the metallic necklace.

Maddie's mission was crystal clear: to create designs that resonate with different girls' personalities. And boy, did she succeed! By the time she turned 13, she had her first million in the bank.

But that's not where this teenage sensation's journey ended. Maddie had bigger dreams and grander ambitions. She boldly stepped onto the stage of "*Shark Tank*," a TV show that's like the Olympics of entrepreneurship. Imagine facing a panel of investors, known as "sharks," and pitching your business idea as a teenager! Maddie faced the sharks and swam among them with grace and charisma.

In a dazzling display of wit and determination, Maddie Bradshaw managed to hook not one, not two, but three "sharks" eager to invest in Snap Caps. This pivotal moment in her life opened up doors to even greater success. With over 2,500 stores in the US and over 30 employees involved in the design, marketing, and sales of her incredible and now diversified line of products, Maddie Bradshaw's bottle cap revolution is an excellent testament that anyone can turn their dreams into a thriving business empire, proving that with hard work, creativity, and passion, anything is possible.

Of course, it helps to understand some basics about personal finance and what it takes to succeed. Understanding the basic pillars of personal finance is a great place to start. They should form the foundation of your journey to success.

ASSETS AND LIABILITIES: YOUR FINANCIAL SEE-SAW

Imagine your money as a giant see-saw. On one side, you've got your assets (the stuff you own worth cash, like your phone, jewelry, or even that vintage video game collection). On the other side, you've got your liabilities (the stuff you owe, like paying back your older sibling for lending you money to buy that exclusive, limited-edition collectible). Keep your see-saw balanced! Subtract what you owe from what you own, and voilà, you've got your net worth (Financial, 2018).

Assets: What's the Scoop?

Assets are like your financial superhero. They can swoop in to save the day when you need cash fast. We're talking about stuff like money in your savings account, your investments, and even the equity in your home. Remember Maddie? She'd been saving every Christmas, tooth fairy, and birthday money. At age 10, she could withdraw a modest sum of $300 to invest in her start- up company. But remember, not everything counts as an asset. Your collection of Angry Birds toys? Sorry, that's a no-go unless someone will pay top dollar for those plush pals. The moral of the story? Be discerning about the things you acquire, the stuff you spend money on, and how much you put away when you need it (Financial, 2018).

Liabilities: The Money Owed Blues

On the flip side, liabilities are like those sneaky villains trying to take your hard-earned cash. They're the debts you owe, like your student loans, mortgage, or credit card balances. And watch out for interest rates; they're like the henchmen of your liabilities, making them grow if you're not careful! You want to avoid having a debt (due to accumulated interest) upon a debt!

INCOME AND EXPENSES: THE MONEY DANCE

Now, let's talk about the day-to-day stuff: your income and expenses. Think of it as a never- ending dance-off between your earnings and your spending.

Income: Cha-Ching!

Income is the money you bring in. If you're a student, it might be your allowance, part-time job paycheck, or that sweet cash from your side hustle selling homemade jewelry. Retirement funds, investments, and even tax refunds also count as income when you're all grown up (Financial, 2018).

Expenses: The Spending Shenanigans

Expenses are the money you shell out for everything, from your cell phone bill to your favorite video games. Keeping track of these can be like trying to herd cats, but it's super important.

Remember, you have to make sure your expenses don't outweigh your income. Don't let those impulse buys throw your budget off-kilter (Financial, 2018)!

Top Tips for Keeping It Cool

- To keep your spending in check, ask yourself if what you want is a "need" or a "want." Take a breather before dipping into your not-so-deep pockets.
- Consider side hustles or creative ways to boost your income, like online surveys, gig work, or even starting an online biz like digital marketing.
- Be wary of retail therapy when you're feeling down; it's a slippery slope!
- Track every penny you spend; there are handy apps for that (Spendee, EveryDollar, Monefy, etc.).

Remember your Four Pillars—Assets, Liabilities, Income, and Expenses—are like your financial GPS. When they're in balance, you're on the right path. But if they're out of whack, it's time for some financial CPR. So, whether you're just starting your financial journey or a budgeting ninja, understanding these Four Pillars is the key to financial freedom (Financial, 2018).

THE TIME VALUE OF MONEY

Fair warning: This concept might sound like a snooze fest, but take my word; it is super important for your money game; understanding the Time Value of Money, or TVM for short, is as important as understanding the Four Pillars.

What Is TVM All About?

Okay, imagine you've got 100 bucks in your pocket right now. You can spend, invest, or leave it under your mattress for a year. What is the best thing to do with it?

Well, Time Value of Money (TVM) says having 100 bucks today is way better than having it in the future if you invest it now. What about the possibility of spending it on something you really want?

The value you can get for those bucks, meaning your consumer or buying power, is better now than it will be a decade from now. Do you know those stories about your Gran and Gramps being able to buy a brand-new Dodge for just over $10,000 in 1970? Well, let's say it's not in the same category as them telling you about how they had to cross over mountains, swim streams, and walk ten thousand miles to get to school; this was true! So, if you choose to spend the $100, know that you can now buy much more with that money than the same amount will get you in the future.

However, if, after reading this book, your best option is to invest your money, well, I am proud of you. You are choosing to make that money work for you, and it will grow over time. It's like a snowball getting bigger as it rolls down a hill. That's the magic of something called compounding interest, and it's like your money's superpower (Fernando, 2023).

In a nutshell, the Time Value of Money principle means that money can grow only through investing, so a delayed investment is a lost opportunity.

So, what you do with every dollar and cent in the here and now is important; fortunes are built one cent at a time, appropriately invested for the long haul. Don't wait. Now is the time to invest in your future success story.

What Is Interest?

Interest is like a reward or a fee you get or pay when you borrow or save money. It's a way for people and banks to make money from money. Let's check out two sides of interest: earning (the fun part) and paying interest (not so fun).

Earning Interest

Imagine you have some money saved up in a bank account. The bank wants to use your money to make loans to other people or businesses because they can earn more money by lending it out than keeping it safe. To encourage you to keep your money in the bank, they offer you a little extra money as a reward. This extra money is called "Interest." It's like the bank saying, "Thanks for letting us use your money, and here's a little extra for you."

But why do they pay you? Well, banks use people's savings and then loan that money to others at a higher interest rate. The difference between what they pay you and what they earn from loans is how they make their profit. So, when you save money, you're helping the bank because they can use your money to make even more money, and so can you.

When many people save money, banks have more to lend out, invest, or buy assets, so they can be picky and offer lower interest to savers. But when people save less, there's also less money to borrow. That's why banks want to encourage people to save more. They offer to pay you a higher interest rate to attract more savers.

It is a bonus to motivate people to keep their money in the bank, which the bank can then loan out at higher interest rates to make even more money.

Paying Interest

Now, let's say you want to buy something big, like a new phone, but you need more money saved up. When you become a grown-up and have a job, you can borrow money from your bank or put it on a credit card (a preapproved loan with a fixed interest rate). When you do this, however, the bank charges you a fee for using their money. This fee is also called "Interest," but in this case, it's not a reward; it's a cost. And the longer it takes to repay the borrowed money, the more interest you'll pay. Depending on the type of loan, this interest can also compound (think about the mortgages folks are being crushed beneath). When interest on debt compounds, unlike the interest on compounding from investments, the money you pay on loans is much higher and compounds faster, making it difficult to pay off. Paying off loans owed is more important than investing first. You will never make more money on investments than the interest and compounding on a loan. That's smart money. It's that see-saw balance.

Simply put, interest can work for you (when you save or invest) or against you (when you borrow). Understanding how it all works can help you make smarter financial decisions.

The TVM Formula: No Need to Panic!

Sure, there's a formula for TVM, but don't worry, it's not rocket science. It considers stuff like future value (how much your money will be worth in the future), present value (what it is worth now), interest rate, compounding periods per year, and the number of years (Fernando, 2023).

Here's the basic formula:

$$FV = PV \times (1 + r/n) ^\wedge (n * t)$$

- FV is the future value of money.
- PV is the present value of money.
- r is the interest rate.
- n is the number of compounding periods per year.
- t is the number of years.

But wait! In real life, things can get more complex with annuities or perpetuity payments, so the formula might have extra bells and whistles.

COOL WAYS TO DEVELOP THE RIGHT MONEY 'TUDE

Wanna slay at the money game? Having the right 'tude towards your moolah can set you on the path to financial awesomeness. We're talking about having that money mindset that makes you feel in control and ready to conquer your financial goals. No cap! So, let's break it down for real (Cueto, 2022)

Visualize Success

Picture this: You're stacking those dollars in your savings account, and it's growing faster than you can say "cash flow." That green you owe your sib? Paid off and feeling fresh! You've even got extra money each month to splurge or be charitable. Are you saving for something special? Set and secured! It's all about seeing the green before it's in your wallet. It's all about setting achievable goals and then working towards them.

Be Hungry to Learn

Whether you're a podcast person or prefer to read up on money stuff, there's a ton of legit resources out there. Check out personal finance websites, budgeting apps, or money-themed podcasts like NPR's Planet Money. Learning about money is like leveling up in a video game; you gain skills and make bank moves.

Chill With Money-Savvy Buds

Life gets much easier when you and your crew are on the same page about money. If you're gonna hang with kids who wanna flex with every dollar they get, that kinda 'tude will not only burn a hole in your pocket as you try to match their spending. All the while, your dreams start to evaporate and seem impossible to achieve. Having buddies who also have lofty money goals and are serious about building up those savings will help you stay on track and strive to achieve those goals.

Create a Budget

Knowing what you'll spend money on and how much you can put away before the money arrives is an excellent way of staying on top of your money game.

Eat Out Less

We know hitting up the local café with your squad is fun, but making breakfast at home and brewing your own Joe is the move. Prepping your meals and snacks isn't just old school; it's a money-saving hack that'll boost your financial street cred.

Weigh Every Decision

Every choice you make can impact your money game. Consider setting a three-month budget; that's like having a game plan. It'll help you decide if that extra splurge is worth it. Make each move wise, and you'll see your savings grow.

Save First, Spend Later

Got big dreams like owning a car, going on that dream vacation, or having a solid emergency fund? Put your savings goals first on your financial checklist. Before you go splurging on takeout, prioritize your savings. It's like securing your bag before a shopping spree.

Start a Journal

Writing down your feelings about money can help you spot any negativity in your mindset and keep you focused on working steadily toward your goals. Don't be afraid to learn from your mistakes and keep moving forward regardless.

Spend and Shop Smarter

Shopping like a pro means using coupons, comparing prices online, and checking for cashback deals. It's not just about saving money; it's about making sure your cash works for you, and being savvy while shopping will leave you with more money in your pocket.

Spend Wisely

Every dollar you spend is another that isn't finding its way into your savings, but you also need balance in life. So, treat yourself now and then, but always remember your goals.

Remember Your Humanity

Try volunteering or giving to charity so that you can positively impact others. It also helps us to develop gratitude for what we have. Life can change in a heartbeat; a homeless person can become rich overnight; a rich man can lose everything with one wrong financial decision. It is so important to keep it real; stay humble and grounded.

EXAMPLES OF COMPOUNDING, PLEASE!

Now that you see more moolah in your account, it's time to make that money work for you. Suppose you have $1,000 to invest for one year at a 10% interest rate compounded annually. The future value of that money is (Fernando, 2023):

$$FV= \$1000 \text{ x } (1 + 0.10/1) \text{ ^ } (1 \text{ x } 1) = \$1,100$$

So, your money grows to $1,100 in a year, Cha-ching!

But if you want to know how much you need to invest today to have $5,000 in a year at a 7% interest rate, the formula flips:

$$PV = \$5,000 / (1 + 0.07/1) \text{ ^ } (1 \text{ x } 1) = \$4,673$$

You'd need to invest $4,673 today to have $5,000 in a year.

To make life easier, there are several online calculators you can use to project what you will end up with after a few years. Try using a realistic amount you know you can invest monthly, say

$10, over two years. Have fun playing around with the numbers to see what is possible.

Compounding Matters

The number of times your money compounds yearly can seriously shake things up—your future value changes if you compound quarterly, monthly, or even daily. Check with your bank about the compounding period of your savings when opening your bank account (we will discuss how to do this later).

Learning about money is a total game changer. It doesn't matter if you're trying to build your emergency fund or want to save towards opening up your little biz on the side; every dollar you put aside brings you closer to turning your dreams into a reality. It starts with knowing the four pillars of personal finance and then developing a winning attitude to your money game. Once you start raking in the moolah, it's time to make that cha-ching in the bank work for you with your compounding knowledge. It also helps to understand how bank charges work so you can avoid unnecessary surprise deductions each month. Wanna test how much you've learned about personal finance? Check out this nifty quiz.

ACTIVITY: PERSONAL FINANCE QUIZ

Alright, let's put your money smarts to the test! Choose the best answer for each question and see how you stack up (*Personal Finance Quiz & Financial Literacy Questions*, n.d.).

1. Why is insurance important?

A) It allows you to share your risk with the insured.
B) It eliminates risk.
C) It makes someone else pay for accidents or losses.
D) Don't know.

2. When it comes to purchasing items, what is the recommended approach?

A) Opt for items with the most benefits.
B) Always choose the least expensive option.
C) Make decisions after comparing costs and benefits.
D) Don't know.

3. Jen and Matt have identical interest-bearing bank accounts earning $10 interest annually. Matt leaves the $10 in the account each year, while Jen takes the $10 home and saves it in a jar without spending any. After five years, who has more money?

A) Jen.
B) Matt
C) They both have the same amount.
D) Don't know.

4. What is a budget?

A) A strict spending limit that cannot be exceeded.
B) A spending plan indicating sources and uses of income.
C) The amount a credit card allows you to charge without penalties.
D) Don't know.

5. During inflation, which is expected to retain its value best?

A) Corporate bond.
B) House.
C) Certificate of deposit.
D) Don't know.

6. Which of the following could negatively affect your credit score?

A) Paying off student loan debt.
B) Closing a long-held credit card.
C) Getting married.
D) Don't know.

7. Historically, which investment has shown the highest rate of return over long periods?

A) Bank savings account.
B) Bonds.
C) Stocks.
D) Don't know.

8. What loan is most likely to be considered "predatory"?

A) High-interest rate on a store credit card.
B) Variable interest rate home mortgage that could rise significantly with inflation.
C) A cashback home loan with a higher interest rate was obtained after a high-pressure sales pitch.
D) Don't know.

9. According to financial experts, what usually provides the best value in automobile ownership?

A) Purchasing a relatively new used car and driving it for a long time.
B) Buying a new car and driving it for a few years.
C) Buying the cheapest used car available.
D) Don't know.

10. Which strategy has historically shown the highest return over time?

A) Frequent movement in and out of the stock market to avoid downturns and take advantage of upturns.
B) Buying and holding onto a diversified set of stocks, ignoring short-run fluctuations.
C) Avoiding stocks entirely, keeping money in federally insured bank accounts.
D) Don't know.

Time to reveal how you did! A score of 8–10 is excellent; 6–7 is average; 5 is not great; 1–4 means we need to up our game—but we will get there.

Here are the correct answers for the quiz:

1. Why is insurance important?

Correct Answer: A) It allows you to share your risk with the insured.

Insurance is crucial because it enables individuals to spread the financial risk of potential accidents or losses. It is a mechanism where policyholders collectively share the burden, providing a safety net for unforeseen events.

2. When it comes to purchasing items, what is the recommended approach?

Correct Answer: C) Make decisions after comparing costs and benefits.

The advisable method when making purchases is to assess and compare the costs and benefits of the items in question. This approach ensures a thoughtful decision-making process that considers value for money.

3. Jen and Matt have identical interest-bearing bank accounts earning $10 interest annually. Matt leaves the $10 in the account each year, while Jen takes the $10 home and saves it in a jar without spending any. After five years, who has more money?

Correct Answer: B) Matt.

Matt accumulates more money over five years because leaving the interest in the account allows for compounding, leading to a higher total than Jen, who removes the interest from the account.

4. What is a budget?

Correct Answer: B) A spending plan indicating sources and uses of income.

A budget is a comprehensive spending plan that outlines the sources of income and how that income will be allocated across various expenses. It serves as a financial guide for effective money management.

5. During inflation, which is expected to retain its value best?

Correct Answer: B) House.

Regarding inflation, real assets like houses retain value better than financial instruments. Real estate often acts as a hedge against inflation, making it a more stable investment during such economic conditions.

6. Which of the following could negatively affect your credit score?

Correct Answer: B) Closing a long-held credit card.

Closing a long-held credit card account can impact your credit score by reducing the average age of your credit accounts, potentially leading to a lower credit score.

7. Historically, which investment has shown the highest rate of return over long periods?

Correct Answer: C) Stocks.

Stocks have historically demonstrated the highest rate of return over extended periods, although they come with higher volatility and risk.

8. What loan is most likely to be considered "predatory"?

Correct Answer: C) Cashback home loan with a higher interest rate obtained after a high- pressure sales pitch.

Predatory loans often involve deceptive practices, and a cashback home loan with unfavorable terms obtained through high-pressure sales tactics is an example of a predatory lending scenario.

9. According to financial experts, what usually provides the best value in automobile ownership?

Correct Answer: A) Purchasing a relatively new used car and driving it for a long time.

Financial experts generally advise that buying a relatively new used car and maintaining it over an extended period offers the best value in terms of depreciation and overall cost of ownership.

10. Which strategy has historically shown the highest return over a period of years?

Correct Answer: B) Buying and holding onto a diversified set of stocks, ignoring short-run fluctuations.

Buying and holding a diversified portfolio of stocks, focusing on long-term growth and ignoring short-term market fluctuations, has historically yielded the highest returns.

Time to Reveal How You Did!

2

SETTING CLEAR AND MEANINGFUL GOALS

Meet Brennan Agranoff, the teen who turned socks into stacks of cash!

BRENNAN PUTS A SOCK IN IT

A regular high school junior, Brennan was an ordinary kid with an extraordinary idea. He noticed something while watching a basketball game at school. All the players were rocking plain old Nike socks. Boring Right? But here's where the magic happened in Brennan's brain. He thought, "What if those socks had cool designs on them?"

So, in 2013, he decided to take action. He didn't just dream; he got to work! First, he spent a whopping six months learning all about how to put awesome designs on socks. That's some serious dedication, folks. Then he did something really cool. He went to his parents and said, "Hey, can I borrow 3,000 bucks?" They said yes, and that's when the sock empire started.

Brennan set up shop right in his garage. Yep, his garage became the sock headquarters! With a bit of help from his family, he got the machines humming, and he started spreading the word on social media.

Fast-forward five years, and HoopSwagg was outgrowing that garage. They built a massive 1500-square-foot building on their property. Brennan, being the creative genius that he was, came up with over 200 unique sock designs all by himself. He had everything from socks that look like melting ice cream to ones with hilarious jokes.

But wait, there's more! Brennan wasn't satisfied with just 200 designs. He bought a competitor and added over 300 more designs to the mix. That's some serious sock power! They were shipping out over 100 orders daily, and he had a team of 18 awesome people helping.

So, here's the scoop: Brennan Agranoff took a simple idea, added a lot of creativity, and turned it into a million-dollar business. He's proof that you don't need to be a grown-up in a fancy suit to make it big. You need a dream, some determination, and a whole lot of cool socks!

Remember Brennan's story the next time you wear a funky pair of socks. Who knows? You might find the next big idea in your sock drawer (How to Become a Teenage Millionaire: 15 Success Stories, 2018).

WHY IT'S TOTALLY LIT TO SET FINANCIAL GOALS: NINE EPIC BENEFITS!

Ever wondered why setting financial goals is the real deal? You're in for a treat because I'm about to break it down for you (Sabrina,

2020). Buckle up because we're diving into the nine epic benefits that'll have you saying, "Goals, where have you been all my life?"

#1: Dreams Need a Game Plan

I'm gonna keep it real with you: Just dreaming about being rich and famous won't cut it. It would help to have a game plan to make those dreams come true. Financial goals are like the secret treasure map that leads you to your goals. Want that shiny new gadget or an epic adventure?

Goals are your GPS!

#2: Get Specific, Get Results

Do you know what's cooler than being vague? Being specific! Setting financial goals forces you to get super clear about what you want. Want a 1000 bucks for that dream concert ticket? Boom, you got it! Being specific helps you reach those money milestones. Each time you're tempted to splurge on unnecessary things, keeping that goal in sight will set you straight. Every dollar spent on other things only prevents you from getting your hands on those tickets.

#3: Crush Debt Like a Pro

Debt is like that annoying boss battle in a video game. But with financial goals, you'll have the ultimate strategy guide. Goals can help you crush debt faster than a superhero. Say goodbye to those student loans or money you owe your older sibling.

#4: Your Money, Your Freedom

Financial goals are your ticket to freedom. They help you take control of your money. Imagine being financially free; no more asking parents for cash, and you call the shots. Goals are your passport to independence.

#5: Stress Less, Live More

Money stress? Ain't nobody got time for that! Setting financial goals reduces stress levels. You'll feel like a Zen master when you control your cash. No more late-night worries about all the stuff you need money for; it's good vibes all the way.

#6: Confidence Booster

Imagine making money moves with confidence. Financial goals give you that swagger. You'll walk like a boss when you know where your money's going and what it's doing. Confidence level: 100!

#7: Achieve Big Things

Want to buy your dream car or travel the world? Financial goals are your VIP pass to significant achievements. They break those huge dreams into bite-sized, achievable chunks. You'll be living the dream in no time.

#8: Save Smart, Spend Smart

Financial goals aren't just about saving; they're about spending smart, too. You'll learn to prioritize what matters most. Fancy sneakers or saving for that epic concert? Goals help you decide like a pro shopper.

#9: Level up Your Future

Is setting financial goals just for now? Nah, it's for your future, too. Those money-smart moves you make today set you up for an epic future. Travel, bling, car, fancy apartment, starting your own business- goals got your back.

So, why is setting financial goals a must for teens? Because it's the ultimate power move. It's like having a cheat code for life's economic challenges. Plans turn your dreams into reality, boost your confidence, and give you the keys to a stress-free, baller future. Start goal-setting today, and you'll be the financial superhero you were born to be!

Disclaimer: No actual cheat codes were used in financial goal-setting.

LEVELING UP YOUR MONEY GAME: SHORT, MEDIUM, AND LONG- TERM FINANCIAL GOALS

All right, my fellow young money masters, let's talk about setting goals to take your finances to the next level. You've probably heard about setting goals, but did you know there are different types? Get ready to dive into the world of short-, medium-, and long-term financial goals; it's like choosing your adventure in the money universe (*Short, Medium, and Long-Term Financial Goals (Video)*, n.d.)!

Short-Term Financial Goals: Quick Wins!

Short-term financial goals are the ones you can achieve in less than a year. Think of these as your quick wins. Need a new phone, saving up for an epic trip with friends, or knocking out a small debt? These goals are your jam! They're usually low risk, meaning you're less likely to lose your hard-earned cash. To conquer them, you only need some budgeting smarts and a safe place to stash your money, like a bank account or trusty money jar.

Medium-Term Financial Goals: Planning for Tomorrow

Medium-term financial goals are like the middle ground. You aim to conquer these in one to five years. Want to cruise around in your dream car, save up for college, or kickstart your own business? These goals are your game plan for tomorrow. They carry moderate risk, meaning there might be some ups and downs along the way. To slay these goals, you'll need to plan your income and expenses and invest some of your cash in flexible options like mutual funds or certificates of deposit.

Long-Term Financial Goals: The Big Dreams!

Now, let's talk about the big dreams: your long-term financial goals. These are the ones that take more than five years to conquer. Dream of owning a house, making the choices you want in the future without worrying that you don't have the capital to pull it off, or leaving a legacy for future generations? These are your high-stakes goals, and they come with some risk. But don't worry, you've got this! To chase these dreams, you'll need to project your income and expenses way ahead and invest your money for the long haul. Think stocks and bonds; they're like the superheroes of long-term investing!

Check Your Understanding: What Type of Goal?

All right, let's put your newfound knowledge to the test. You want to save money for your mom's birthday gift. Is this a short-, medium-, or long-term goal?

- Choice A) Short-term goal
- Choice B) Medium-term goal
- Choice C) Long-term goal

You got this, money champ! Setting short--, medium---, and long-term financial goals is your secret weapon for conquering the world of finance. It's like building your own money empire, one goal at a time.

STEP 1: THE POWER OF SMART GOALS

You don't have to be a genius to set SMART goals, but it takes this incredible strategy to level up our money game. These goals will have you saying, "*I got this!*" So, let's dive deeper into the power of being SMART when setting your financial goals (Benve, 2023).

S for Specific

Specificity is like your financial compass. It means you need to be ultra-clear about what you want to achieve. Start with the "what". What's the goal? Is it paying off debt, saving for a new gadget, or investing in your future?

Then ask yourself, "Why?" why does it matter to you? Understanding the "why" behind your goal gives it purpose and motivation. Finally, get into the "how;" how will you make it happen? This is where you outline the actionable steps you'll take. So, instead of a vague goal like "*I want to pay off debt,*" go all in with "*I'm gonna crush my $500 cell phone upgrade by saving the money from my side hustle toward it.*"

M for Measurable

Numbers, numbers, numbers! It would help if you quantified your goals. It's not enough to say you want to save or pay off debt; you've got to set a specific value and criteria to measure your progress. You should know when you've nailed it and by how much. Why? Because having clear achievement indicators keeps you focused and accountable. So, forget about the "*I'll save as much as I can*" approach. Instead, say, "*I'll save $500 for my new gaming console in the next four months.*" Now, you've got a clear target to hit.

A for Attainable

Let's talk about attainability. While it's cool to aim high, your goals should still be within reach using your available skills and resources. Think of it as finding the sweet spot between challenge and feasibility. You want your goals to stretch you a bit, but not to the point where they feel impossible. So, saying "*I'll be a millionaire by next year*" might be a bit of a stretch, but "*I'll save $2,000 this year by setting aside $6 a day*" is more on point. It's challenging but doable.

R for Realistic

Being realistic is all about keeping it real. Your goals should align with your skills, resources, and current situation. Setting yourself up for failure with wildly unrealistic goals isn't cool. On the flip side, don't set the bar too low. Realistic goals should require effort but remain within reach. To be realistic, you need to consider both your limitations and capabilities. For instance, "*By managing my finances well, next year,* I'll have enough saved up to move out" might be a tad too ambitious. A more realistic version could be, "*By managing my finances better, in three years, when I am a senior, I'll be able to move out on my own after graduating high school.*"

T for Timely

Time is money, and it's essential to establish a timeframe for financial goals. A deadline adds a sense of urgency and helps you stay consistent. Your timeframe should be measurable, attainable, and realistic. So, "*I'll save* $1,000 for my dream vacation by the end of next summer" is a great example. It's specific about the amount, has a clear endpoint (the end of summer), and is achievable if you plan correctly.

STEP 2: DREAM BIG AND GET CREATIVE

All right, let's fire up those imagination engines! When it comes to dreaming up your financial goals, think of it as making a super cool wish list for your future money (Benve, 2023):

The Long Term: Let's dream big! Imagine yourself 10 to 20 years from now. What would make you feel like a total financial boss? Maybe it's owning your dream home, having the financial freedom to travel the world, starting your own killer business, or living that super adventurous life. These long-term goals set the stage for your epic money journey.

The Medium Term: Now, zoom in a bit. Think about the next one to five years. What are the cool things you want to achieve in this kind of near future? You may be saving up for college, building a safety net fund, crushing that annoying debt, or aiming to score your dream car or a cozy crib. These stepping stones will help you reach those epic long-term dreams.

The Short Term: Let's get even closer to the present, talkin' about next year. What's popping on your radar for the immediate future? Are you planning an incredible vacation, eyeing the latest gadgets, on a mission to slay that credit card debt, or stoked to pick up a new skill? These short- term goals keep your money game strong and your motivation sky-high.

The Right Now: Time to focus on the next 90 days. What's coming up super soon? Are you thinking about kickstarting a little snowball investment early, grabbing a rad business opportunity, treating yourself to something epic like a new gaming console, or leveling up your sneaker collection? These are the goals that make sure you're taking action right here, right now.

STEP 3: MAKE A GAME PLAN

Planning is where the real magic goes down! For each goal, it's time to roll up those sleeves and do some money math. Here's how to make it happen (Benve, 2023):

Calculate the Monthly Savings: Break down those big goals into bite-sized chunks. Figure out how much cash you gotta stash away each month to achieve those big dreams. This is where your game plan comes to life. For example, if your goal is to save $1,000 for an epic summer vacation in a year, you'd need to save around $83 each month ($1,000 divided by 12 months).

This helps you see exactly how much moolah you need to hustle for.

Pay Yourself First: Make saving a non-negotiable part of your money moves. Set up auto- transfers from your checking account to your savings stash right after your money hits your account. This way, you're putting your money goals front and center before considering spending on other stuff.

Stay Committed: Think of your goals like your treasure map to financial awesomeness. Stick to your plan, and always remember why you started this money quest in the first place. It's all about staying dedicated to your dreams and taking action like a boss.

STEP 4: KEEP THE MOMENTUM GOING

Consistency is the name of the game! To make sure you're cruising towards your goals, follow these steps (Benve, 2023):

Create a Progress Report: Every 90 days, do a quick check-in on your goals. Make a simple chart or a super chill spreadsheet with your goals, how much you've saved so far, and when you wanna reach 'em. This progress report helps you see if you're crushing it ahead of schedule or need to make some tweaks.

Stay Flexible: Life can throw some curveballs, and priorities can flip. If you need to catch up on a goal or something unexpected pops up, it's all good; be flexible. Adjust your game plan as needed, but always keep sight of those important goals.

Celebrate the Wins: Remember to give yourself major props along the way! Whether it's hitting a savings milestone, knocking out a chunk of debt, or reaching a financial goal ahead of schedule, take a second to high-five yourself. It's all about staying motivated and keeping that positive vibe.

STEP 5: SHARE THE MONEY JOURNEY

Money goals are way more fun when you bring your squad along (Benve, 2023):

Get Your Fam or Squad on Board: Talk to your family or those you trust about your financial goals. Share why these goals matter and how reaching them benefits everyone. When your family or support system is on the same page, it's easier to work together on the money mission.

Explain the Why: If your goals mean making changes or sacrifices, break down why they're important. Whether cutting back on weekend spending or making smarter choices, explaining the "why" helps everyone understand why it's worth it.

Party Together: When you hit those money milestones or conquer a big goal, celebrate as a team! It's a rad way to show how financial responsibility and teamwork pay off.

So there you have it: your guide to rocking your financial goals like a true champ. Remember, your money dreams are totally doable when you're SMART about it; make a sweet plan, stay committed, and bring your squad along for the ride. You've totally got this!

ALIGNING GOALS WITH VALUES

Budgeting might not sound like the most exciting thing, but guess what? You've got the power to make it work for you in a way that feels natural and not all restricting. Here's the deal (Tim, 2020):

Step 1: Get to Know the Money Game

Budgeting isn't about sticking to someone else's rules. It's more about finding what works for you. So, forget the cash-in-an-envelope stuff if it's not your vibe. You're in control here!

Step 2: Choose Your Money Principles

You don't need to follow a strict budgeting rulebook. Pick the money principles that make sense to you. Don't let anyone tell you otherwise. It's your financial journey, after all.

Step 3: Make It Yours

Now, let's put those chosen money principles into action. I'll walk you through how to make your budget truly your own.

In a nutshell, it's all about building a budget that suits you like your favorite pair of jeans. You've got this!

Here's a rundown of some key principles (Tim, 2020):

1. Percentage-Based Budgeting

This method allows you to allocate a percentage of your income to various categories. For instance, you can decide that 50% of your income goes to needs (V-bucks and iTunes), 30% to saving (for future goals), and 20% to fun activities. The great thing is that you can customize these percentages to suit your priorities and financial goals. It helps ensure you're balancing spending and saving.

2. Everything is Spending

This principle shifts your mindset to see all financial actions as spending, saving, or paying bills. For teens who enjoy spending, this reframing can help you manage your money more effectively. It emphasizes that even saving is a form of spending, but it's an investment in your future.

3. Budget for Every Possible Category

Get a detailed budget by breaking down expenses into specific categories. For example, instead of having a general "entertainment" category, you might separate it into "dining out with friends" and "dates with your crush." This detailed approach helps you understand precisely where your money is going and enables you to make adjustments more easily.

4. Cash Only Principle

This is a straightforward concept: Use physical cash for spending whenever possible. It makes you more aware of your expenses and helps prevent impulse purchases. Keeping a small buffer in your checking account for online payments or emergencies is essential if you adopt this approach.

5. Envelope Budgeting

Envelope budgeting is like the cash-only principle but in a digital form. You assign specific budgets to virtual envelopes or budgeting apps. Once an envelope is empty, you can only spend more in that category during the next budgeting period. It adds discipline to your spending habits.

6. Group Categories Together

Simplify your budget by combining similar expenses into broader categories. For instance, group "groceries" and "personal care items" into one category called "Essentials." This approach streamlines your budget, especially if you don't want to track too many individual expenses.

7. Give Every Dollar a Job

Ensure that every dollar you earn has a specific purpose in your budget. This principle helps you avoid leftover money, ensuring every cent goes toward a financial goal or expense category. It prevents unnecessary spending.

8. Treat Saving Like a Bill

Make saving a non-negotiable part of your budget by treating it as a monthly bill. Assign a specific amount to your savings account just like you would with rent or utilities. This disciplined approach helps you consistently save for your financial goals.

9. Advance Planning Principle

Plan your spending before you even receive your paycheck or allowance. For instance, you can create a list of bills and expenses you anticipate for the upcoming month. When your income arrives, you already have a clear plan for where it should go.

10. Record Every Transaction as it Happens

Use budgeting apps or tools to record your expenses in real time. Whenever you make a purchase, log it immediately. This way, you can keep a close eye on your budget and avoid overspending.

11. The Flexible Budget Principle

This principle allows you to move money between budget categories when needed. For example, if you overspend in one category, you can subtract from another to stay within your budget. It offers flexibility while ensuring you stay within your total spending limit.

12. Never See the Money You Squirrel Away

Set up your finances so that money designated for specific goals, like savings or investments, goes directly into separate accounts. This way, you never see this money in your spending account, reducing the temptation to spend it impulsively.

13. Balance Living for Today with Saving for Tomorrow

Striking a balance between enjoying your present life and saving for future goals is crucial. Don't overspend today to the point of financial stress, but don't neglect saving for your future needs, like your first car or motorcycle.

14. Simplify. Simplify. Simplify.

Make your budget as straightforward as possible. Automate bill payments and savings contributions to save time and reduce the chance of forgetting payments. Simplicity can make budgeting more manageable, especially for busy teens.

Budgeting doesn't have to be dull. Choose the principles that resonate with your financial goals and personality, and you'll be well on your way to managing your money effectively and achieving your financial aspirations.

SET YOUR SMART FINANCIAL GOALS

Try giving this worksheet a whirl if there is something you would like to start saving for (*Setting a SMART Savings Goal SAVINGS CHECKING Accounts*, n.d.).

The Example

Sarah would like to turn heads with her dress at the Prom, but she knows her folks don't have that kind of money to finance her dream evening. So, she decided to finance as much of it as possible by saving up her income from working part-time at the local pizza place. Here is her game plan.

SMART Goal Aspects	Questions	Sarah's SMART Goal
S = Specific	Why are you saving?	Prom costs.
M = Measurable	What is your target?	$500
A = Attainable	How can you do this in time?	Yes, if I earn more; spend less.
R = Relevant	How important is this to you?	Highly: Prom is a once-in-a-lifetime event.
T = Timebound	When will you meet the goal?	In six months and one week (25 weeks)

Sarah's Targets

Sarah wants to save $500; it will take 25 weeks to do it if she saves $20 each week.	**$500 (total amount) ÷ 25 (weeks) = $20/ week**

Sarah's Action Plan

Sarah decided to minimize her spending by bringing snacks from home instead of buying them ($5/week); she will pick up an extra shift on Sundays ($15).

SMART GOAL TEMPLATES

Use the following templates to plot your important savings goals (*Setting a SMART Savings Goal SAVINGS CHECKING Accounts,* n.d.).

SMART Goal Aspects	Questions	Your Savings Goal
S = Specific	Why are you saving?	
M = Measurable	What is your target?	
A = Attainable	How will you do this?	
R = Relevant	Is this important to you?	
T = Timebound	When will you meet your target?	

Your Savings Target

Use this simple formula to calculate how much you'll need to save each week to meet your savings goal.

If I want to save $(total savings) ÷ in weeks = $_/*week*

Rephrase Your Goal as a SMART Goal

Create a detailed SMART goal using the above information in a sentence or two. Pin it up in a place of prominence in your room to keep you motivated.

Your Action Plan

List the steps you will take to meet your weekly savings target. Try to include how much you will save with each step. Remember to factor in unavoidable expenses. Remember to be realistic and practical about what you can do.

Step	Action	Projected Savings
1.		
2.		
3.		
4.		
5.		
	Total savings ($)	

Now that you have grasped the importance of setting attainable financial goals, armed with the right attitude and money-savvy know-how, you are ready for the next stage of your journey: budgeting. You may be surprised to learn that proper budgeting takes a high level of skills and a great deal of thought to make it actionable and achievable.

3

BUILDING A BUDGET FROM SCRATCH

Before you say it, I know the word "budget" has most teens (and a fair share of grown-ups) running for the hills. But in this chapter, I promise we will break it down into manageable steps. To kick things off, check out this crazy story that will hit you in the feels (Lodge, 2019).

HART MAIN'S EPIC JOURNEY: HOW A TEEN TURNED TEASING INTO A CANDLE EMPIRE

When Hart Main was just 13, he playfully teased his sister about her girly scented candles. But what started as a joke turned into a wild idea when Hart wanted to buy a $1,500 bike. "*Why not make cool candles?*" he thought, and ManCans was born.

Hart and his parents pooled their cash to kickstart the project, crafting candles from old soup cans with a seriously dude-like vibe. They came in flavors like Campfire, Bacon, Sawdust, Fresh Cut Grass, and Grandpa's Pipe, the ultimate man-cave accessories.

ManCans are even more remarkable because they're handcrafted by an awesome team at the Beaver Creek Candle Company in Ohio, including folks with developmental disabilities. By 2016, ManCans were everywhere, raking in serious cash, but it wasn't just about money for Hart.

He's got a huge heart, too. Hart donates a slice of every sale to soup kitchens in Ohio, Pennsylvania, West Virginia, and Michigan. So, Hart Main's story isn't just about candles; it's proof that even we teens can do big things and make a difference!

BUDGETING BASICS: HOW TO MAKE MONEY MOVES AND STILL HAVE FUN

So, you might be dealing with boring stuff like geometry and geography in school, but here's some real-world knowledge you won't learn in the classroom: budgeting. Yeah, I know it sounds snoozeworthy, but trust me, it's the key to unlocking financial awesomeness. Check out these rad tips on budgeting like a pro, and you'll be on your way to growing your money stash while still having a blast (Mint, 2022).

Show Me the Money!

First things first, you gotta know how much cash you're raking in. Add it all up, whether from a part-time gig or your monthly allowance for being the family's resident superhero. That's your starting point for baller budgeting. If it fluctuates, play it safe and go with the lower amount.

Category Craze

Now, let's get organized. Split your budget into two main squads: saving and spending. Under these, list all the places your money's gonna go. Here's a sneak peek:

Saving:

Savings account College fund

Cool stuff (like a car or a gaming console) Rainy Day moolah

Spending:

- **Must-haves:** gas, phone bill, lunch money
- **Nice-to-haves:** gym membership, streaming services, snacks
- **Fun stuff:** clothes, makeup, hangouts, entertainment

If you're lucky and don't have to worry about bills like rent and utilities (thanks, parents!), skip 'em. But if you're pitching in, include them as necessary expenses.

Pick Your Budgeting Style

Time to choose your budgeting weapon. There are a few ways to do it:

- **"Pay Yourself First":** Stick some money in savings first, then spend what's left.
- **Zero-based budgeting:** Make sure every dollar has a job, even if it's just chilling in savings.

- **50/30/20 Rule:** Split your cash into 50% for essentials, 30% for fun, and 20% for savings. Adjust as needed.

Save First, Splurge Later

Listen up, it's a golden rule: always put money in savings before spending. If you go on a spending spree first, you might blow your budget. Saving first builds discipline and keeps you on track.

Set Goals

Got dreams? Saving helps you reach 'em. Having goals makes budgeting much cooler, whether for a special occasion or a killer ride. Check out the previous chapter for a refresher on setting those SMART goals.

Track Your Moves

Keep tabs on your spending. Use a habit tracker to see where your money's going. If you find yourself dropping stacks on fancy coffee, swap it for a homemade brew and watch your budget grow.

Tweak Your Budget

If your budget's feeling off, change it. If you're always short on gas money, adjust. And if you've got extra cash, find somewhere cool to stash it.

Learn From Oopsies

Mistakes happen. Did you miss your savings goal and have to skip a hangout? Reflect on what went wrong and do better next time. Good money habits come with practice.

Side Hustle Swagger

Want more cash? Get a side hustle. You can do stuff like start a podcast, pet-sit, bake and sell treats, or even tutor others. Cha-ching!

Minimalist Money Moves

Less spending equals more money in the bank. Try a capsule wardrobe (fewer clothes, more style), buy secondhand, and get creative with what you already have.

No Peer Pressure

Don't let peer pressure mess with your budget. Real friends will hang out wherever; no fancy stuff is required.

Seek Wisdom

It's okay to ask for help. Talk to your parents or financial gurus for advice. Read books or listen to podcasts about money. Knowledge is power.

Tech and Social Media FTW

Budgeting can be fun, especially with tech and social media. Use apps like Empower to manage your budget. Check out YouTube videos to learn financial lingo and hacks.

Follow Money-Savvy Influencers

Hit up social media for financial inspiration. TikTok stars are breaking down money concepts in quick videos. Learn from the pros and level up your money game.

Budgeting might seem boring, but it's the secret sauce to financial freedom. So, start young, budget like a pro, and live your best life without breaking the bank!

NEEDS, WANTS, AND MOOLAH

Just the word "budgeting" may sound like a lullaby to teens, but trust me, it's the secret sauce to handling your money. One of the first things you want to understand is the difference between needs and wants (Lee, 2021).

Needs are like the must-haves in life. Think of them as the essentials for survival, like food, water, a place to live, clothes, and safety. You know, the basics you can't live without.

Wants, on the other hand, are like nice-to-haves. They're all the cool stuff you desire, but you could totally live without them. It's like that extra-large pizza, those designer sneakers, or that fancy bedroom with a private bathroom.

But here's the tricky part: sometimes, your brain might try to convince you that a want is actually a need. You might see your friends rocking the latest iPhone or flaunting a designer hoodie, and suddenly, you feel like you *need* one, too. It happens to the best of us!

Why is it crucial to know the difference between needs and wants, you ask? Here's the deal: understanding this difference is like a superpower for wisely handling your money.

Imagine facing a tough choice: Do you want one marshmallow now or two marshmallows later? It's a bit like the famous "marshmallow test," where kids who could wait for the bigger reward showed self-discipline. For teens, it's about choosing between immediate splurging and saving for bigger long-term goals.

Knowing the distinction between needs and wants is the first step in building money skills. As you grow into adulthood, you'll need to create budgets and make decisions like paying rent before booking that dream vacation with your pals.

So, here are four excellent ways to learn and remember the needs vs. wants lesson (Lee, 2021):

- **Get Hands-On:** Take out that dusty Monopoly board and play with Monopoly money. Allocate it to different categories like rent, groceries, and fun stuff. Then, see how much is left for your wants. It'll make budgeting feel real!
- **Volunteer:** Help those in need to appreciate what you have. Organize a food drive, volunteer at a shelter, or tutor younger kids. It's not only a kind thing to do, but it also helps you understand the real needs in life.
- **Take Charge:** Empower yourself by paying for your own wants. Cover the cost of your coffee shop trips or video games with your own cash. It teaches you to make choices and breaks the "Bank of Mom and Dad" cycle.
- **Talk It Out:** Have open conversations about money with your parents or support system. Ask questions, discuss your values, and research your purchases. Is that cool gadget a want or a need? Do your homework before spending your hard-earned cash.

BUDGETING APPS

One more awesome tool to help you manage your money: budgeting apps. They're a great way to practice managing your needs and wants safely and securely (Colestock, 2023).

For Your Young Sibs (Aged 3-12):

- **Rooster Money:** This app is super cool for families. It helps you learn about spending, saving, and even giving money to charity. Plus, it has a free version!
- **PiggyBot:** This one helps you figure out how much money you have and how close you are to your savings goals. It's free, too!
- **Allowance+:** If you want to track your allowance and spending, this app can help. It's free, and you can use it on multiple devices.

For Teens (Ages 13-18):

- **Bankaroo:** This app is like virtual banking for teens. It's excellent for tracking money, setting goals, and planning future expenses. There are both free and paid versions.
- **Gohenry:** With this app, you get your very own debit card (with parental controls, of course) to spend money and learn about financial stuff. It's about $3.99 per month.
- **BusyKid:** This app does everything: earning, saving, budgeting, and investing. And it's free!
- **Greenlight:** This app is for you if you're into chore lists and allowances. It teaches you about spending choices and costs around $4.99 monthly for up to five kids.

For Young Adults (Ages 18+):

- **FamZoo:** This app is awesome for older teens and young adults. It helps you manage money, set goals, and plan for expenses. Prices range from $2.50 to $5.99 per month.

- **Acorns:** You might have heard of this one. It's great for saving, investing, and planning for your future. It costs about $5 per month.

So, there you have it! Understanding needs vs. wants is your ticket to becoming a money-savvy winner. Budget wisely, save smartly, and remember, you've got the power to make your financial dreams come true!

THE 50/30/20 BUDGET

Ready to level up your money game? We're about to explore the super cool 50/30/20 Rule, your secret weapon for mastering budgeting. Let's break it down with examples (VanSomeren, n.d.)!

What's the 50/30/20 Rule?

Think of the 50/30/20 Rule as your budgeting sidekick. It's a simple guideline that helps you split your money into three categories (VanSomeren, n.d.):

1. **50% for Needs:** These are the must-haves in your life. Imagine you're on a deserted island, and you can only bring the essentials: food (groceries), shelter (rent or housing), and power (utilities like electricity and water). Remember your car insurance; it's your superhero shield against unexpected road hazards!
2. **30% for Wants:** These are the fun parts of life that make you smile. Picture this: you're planning an epic day out with friends, grabbing your favorite snacks, catching a movie, and splurging on the latest video game or concert tickets. These are the things you love but could survive without.

3. **20% for Financial Goals:** This is your treasure chest for the future. Imagine saving up for that epic road trip with your pals or stashing away money for college. It's also where you tackle any debts, like the money you owe for that impressive smartphone you bought.

Why Does It Work?

The 50/30/20 Rule is your budgeting secret sauce because (Van-Someren, n.d.):

- It helps you take charge of your spending.
- It stops you from going overboard on splurges.
- It's as simple as leveling up in your favorite video game.

How to Use the 50/30/20 Rule for Budgeting

Step 1: Calculate Your Monthly Income

Add up all the money you make each month, like your allowance or any cash from a part-time job. If you save money for later (like in a piggy bank), include that too.

Step 2: Set Your Spending Targets

For Needs: Half of your income (50%) is for the gotta-haves.

For Wants: Three out of every ten bucks (30%) are for the fun stuff.

For Financial Goals: One-fifth (20%) goes into your savings and paying off any debts.

Step 3: Plan Your Budget

Think of these three categories as pockets for your cash. List what you spend your money on in the right pocket and check if you're sticking to your targets.

Example Time!

Imagine you have a monthly income of $300:

Needs: You should spend $150 (50%) on stuff like food, your phone, and maybe helping with some bills at home or gas money.

Wants: That's $90 (30%) for fun outings, gaming, or treating yourself to snacks and cool stuff.

Financial Goals: Put $60 (20%) into your savings, like a jar for future adventures or paying off any money you owe.

It can be mind-boggling to think about budgeting for the whole month. It helps to break it down into weekly and then daily amounts. For example, weekly savings would break down to $15 a week, meaning you will save about $2 and some change daily.

In the "Wants" category, you're looking at $90 per month, which means you can allow yourself to indulge by treating yourself to the tune of $22.50 per week on outings and non-essentials.

A Few Things to Keep In Mind

The 50/30/20 Rule is a guide, not a strict rule. Adjust it to fit your own money adventure.

It won't work like magic; you've got to keep an eye on your spending to make sure you're staying on track.

Explore Other Budgeting Methods

While the 50/30/20 rule rocks, there are other ways to budget. Some teens go for the 80/20 rule, where you save 20% right off the bat. Or you could try the 70/20/10 Rule, splitting your cash into living expenses, saving, and spending.

Ready to become a budgeting champ or a teen superhero? The 50/30/20 Rule is your secret weapon to conquer your money goals. Start today, and you'll be on your way to becoming a money-savvy legend!

Remember, money advice can change based on your unique situation, so consider chatting with a money pro if you have specific questions.

DELAYED GRATIFICATION LEADS TO FINANCIAL SUCCESS

Have you ever had to choose between spending money on something cool right now or saving up for something even more remarkable in the future? It's a dilemma we all face, and today, we're going to dive into a magical concept called "delayed gratification" that can make you a money wizard (Wall Strategies, 2020)!

What's Delayed Gratification?

Picture this: You're given the choice between daily Uber rides to school or saving that money and going on a fantastic European vacation at the end of the month. Europe, right? But we often pick instant fun and convenience over long-term goals in real life. We grab those late-night snacks when we want to get healthier or spend cash on stuff we don't really need instead of saving or investing it. That's where delayed gratification comes in!

Delayed Gratification Is Your Superpower

Delayed gratification is like your secret weapon. It means resisting the temptation of immediate pleasures to snag bigger rewards down the road (Wall Strategies, 2020). Think of it as choosing two marshmallows later instead of one right now (like in that famous experiment). Turns out your ability to delay gratification can predict your success in life!

So, why is it awesome for your money journey?

1. Saving for Bigger Adventures

Imagine this: Instead of splurging on small things daily, you stash away that cash. You could buy an incredible espresso machine, make coffee at home, and save money for years! Cook more, eat out less, and that money could fund your dream trip or even help you buy your own place someday. Delayed gratification lets you say "no" to small temptations for "yes" to big, exciting goals. For instance, if you spent less than $90 on your wants for one month, you would have $180 after two months or $360 after four! Think about how much closer to achieving your goals you could get with a bit of sacrifice here and there.

2. Growing Your Money

Here's the money magic: Money grows over time! It's like planting a seed that becomes a money tree. When you save or invest, your money earns interest and keeps growing. If you spend that dollar instead, you miss out on all its future potential. Seriously, your money can turn into three dollars in 28 years if it grows at a 4% yearly rate. That's like turning pocket change into treasure! Here's a much more incredible example: saving $10 a week at 4% interest would be $24,512.63 in 28 years! Using the average interest rate in the stock market of 10% per year, if you decided to invest $10 a week ($1.43 a day), it could be $73,386 in 28 years compounded monthly! The choice of how to grow your money is entirely yours.

Becoming a Delayed Gratification Pro

Now, how can you get better at this superpower?

Tip 1: Get in Your Best Shape

Taking care of yourself through healthy eating, getting enough sleep, and exercising actually boosts your willpower. It's like filling up your "say no to temptation" tank!

Tip 2: Focus on Goals

Keep your goals in sight! Visualizing what you're saving for makes it easier to stick to your plan. Keep that dream alive, whether it's a dream vacation, a cool gadget, or even college! Designing a vision board and placing it in a strategic spot you see every day will keep your eyes on the prize.

Tip 3: Hang with the Right Crowd

We're influenced by the people around us. It's tough to resist if your friends are about spending recklessly. So, surround yourself with pals who also aim for big goals. It's easier when you're all in it together!

Remember: Balance Is Key

While delayed gratification is terrific, remember to enjoy life in the moment, too! Saving doesn't mean living off canned beans and being miserable. The goal is to have a fantastic life both now and later. Find that perfect balance, and you'll rock your money journey!

So, there you have it, your superpower to conquer money goals: Delayed Gratification! Start using it today, and you'll be on your way to becoming a money-savvy legend.

Money advice can vary based on your unique situation, so chat with a money pro if you have specific questions. Go out there and make your money moves!

ACTIVITY: BUDGET QUIZ

Take this unique quiz to uncover your spending and budgeting tendencies. Answer honestly to discover what kind of money person you are.

Imagine you receive your monthly allowance. What's your first thought?

a) Time to save some of it for future goals.
b) I'll spend some and save some for later.
c) Let's treat myself and spend it all!

It's the end of the month, and you have $20 left from your allowance. What do you do?

a) Add it to your savings or invest in something you care about.
b) Keep it in your wallet as spare cash.
c) Splurge on something you've been eyeing.

When you want to buy a new gadget or fashion item, how do you make the decision?

a) Research, compare prices, and save until you can afford it.
b) Buy it impulsively if you have enough money at the moment.
c) Borrow money or use a credit card to get it ASAP.

Do you have a part-time job or engage in any money-earning activities?

a) Yes, I work part-time or do freelance gigs.
b) No job, but I occasionally earn money through odd jobs.
c) I rely solely on my allowance or my parents for money.

How often do you check your bank account or keep track of your spending?

a) Regularly, I track every expense and income.
b) Occasionally, I check when I think about it.
c) Rarely, I prefer not knowing the exact numbers.

Results:

Mostly A's - Financial Planner

You're a financial planner! You excel at managing your money, saving for the future, and making informed financial decisions. Keep up the excellent work!

Mostly B's - Balanced Budgeter

You're a balanced budgeter. You have some good financial habits but could benefit from a bit more discipline and planning. Explore ways to improve your budgeting skills.

Mostly C's - Spontaneous Spender

You tend to be a spontaneous spender. It's time to consider the importance of budgeting and financial planning. Explore resources to help you gain better control over your finances.

This quiz should provide insight into your financial habits and inspire you to change your money management approach positively!

Now that we have a solid budget and saving strategy in place, we should set our sights on setting up our checking accounts or other banking tools and products.

4

AN INTRODUCTION TO CHECKING ACCOUNTS

ALINA'S LOLLIPOP DREAM: FROM TOOTH-FRIENDLY TREATS TO MULTI-MILLION DOLLAR SUCCESS

Alina, at the age of seven, was given a lollipop by a bank teller. Inspired to create a lollipop that's good for teeth, she launched Zollipops in 2014. These 100% natural, vegan, and sugar-free lollipops were a hit. Alina expanded her Zolli Candy brand to include tooth-friendly taffy, gummies, and caramels. Zolli Candy became a multi-million-dollar company and made Inc.'s list of fastest-growing private companies. The takeaway? Follow your dreams, work hard, and you can achieve sweet success! (Squad, 2021)

WHY YOU SHOULD HAVE A BANK ACCOUNT

Having a bank account is like a boss move on your way to financial freedom and keeping your money safe. It might seem intimidating, but it's a legit step that sets you up for financial success. Check out these six reasons why having a bank account is a must for teens and young adults (*Why Teens Should Open a Bank Account*, n.d.).

1. **Money Freedom:** Getting a bank account means taking control of your cash, which is a big step towards being financially independent. It helps you see how your money connects to your daily spending. Think of it like this: It's like leveling up your skills to handle college expenses or save for that sweet ride. Plus, you get to decide how much money goes into savings or credit accounts, making your money work for you with that interest bonus.
2. **Necessity and Convenience:** A bank account is a must when you start making those hard- earned bucks, even from your side hustle. You can set up direct deposit, so all the cash you make goes straight into your account. No more shady payday lenders or cash-checking places taking a piece of your money. A bank account lets you quickly deposit cash, take out money, shop online, and pay bills. Say goodbye to carrying loads of cash or using sketchy apps.
3. **Building Your Money Credit:** Your bank account is the foundation of your credit history. Managing it responsibly by keeping a positive balance and paying bills on time opens doors for getting loans or renting an apartment later. Unlike those money-sharing apps (good for splitting bills with pals), banks are where your actions build a killer credit score.
4. **Safety and Security:** Your bank account is like a vault for your money. It's also backed by the FDIC, a federal agency that ensures your money is safe, even if your bank goes under. So, no need to worry about losing or damaging your cash. It's way more reliable than some money-sharing apps with iffy insurance.

5. **Budgeting and Money Skills:** Banks make it easy to track your spending and stick to a budget. Most have online banking and cool mobile apps to help you check your account and stay on top of your money game. Plus, they offer loads of resources and programs to help you become a money master.
6. **Saving and Future Plans:** Your bank account isn't just for spending; it's your secret weapon for saving and planning for your epic future. Some accounts can set up automatic savings, so your money grows over time.

Check this out; some checking accounts even offer interest, which means your money is making more money. Apps and programs help you set savings goals and work towards them. You set up a bright financial future by building a solid financial history, a strong credit score, and a chill relationship with banks.

So, getting a bank account might not be the most exciting thing ever. Still, it's a key step toward securing your financial future. And remember, before making any big money decisions, it's wise to talk to a parent, guardian, or trusted adult for guidance. Your journey to financial success starts right here, and by taking this step, you're setting yourself up for major success. Keep hustling!

HOW TO OPEN A BANK ACCOUNT

Now that you understand the importance of having a bank account. Let's dive into the steps to open one (*How to Open a Bank Account as a Teen*, n.d.):

Step 1: Choose the Right Bank

Selecting the right bank is crucial. There are three primary types of banks to consider:

1. **Commercial Banks:** These are the most common and offer a wide range of services, including checking and savings accounts, loans, and credit cards. Notable examples are Bank of America and Wells Fargo.
2. **Credit Unions:** These non-profit organizations are owned and governed by their members. They provide similar services to commercial banks but typically offer lower fees and better rates. The Navy Federal Credit Union and State Employees Credit Union are examples.
3. **Online Banks:** While lacking physical branches, online banks provide many services akin to commercial banks. They may offer higher savings account interest rates and lower fees. Notable online banks include Ally Bank and Capital One 360.

Step 2: Research and Consider Features

Selecting the right bank involves thorough research. The Consumer Financial Protection Bureau offers helpful resources. Assess what features matter most to you. Do you need a checking or savings account? Is easy access to ATMs a priority? Consider any account opening fees and minimum balance requirements.

Also, evaluate the bank's community involvement. You can research banks and credit unions in your area to find one with a strong history of serving and supporting your community. Visiting the bank in person can provide valuable insights.

Step 3: Prepare for Application

Once you've chosen your bank or credit union, you'll need to apply for an account, which involves some paperwork. Fortunately, the documentation required is similar to what you'd need for employment. The specific documents can vary, so consult a bank employee for precise information. In general, you'll need

- a valid form of ID (such as a driver's license, passport, or state ID card).
- your Social Security Number (SSN) or taxpayer identification number (TIN).
- proof of address, like a utility bill or lease agreement.
- proof if you're under 18, a school ID.
- an initial deposit to open the account.
- proof if you're under 18, a parent or guardian's signature, and ID.
- additional documentation if your account has a minimum balance requirement.

For those under 18, some banks may offer a "non-custodial" account for 16 or 17-year-olds who can provide identification and proof of income.

Step 4: Get Banked!

Once approved, you'll need to deposit money into your account to open it. Familiarize yourself with the account's features, such as making deposits, withdrawing money, and checking your balance. Understand any associated fees and learn how to avoid them. Bank professionals are there to guide you through this process.

Your financial journey begins with these essential steps, laying the groundwork for a secure and prosperous future. As always, when making significant financial decisions, it's wise to consult with a parent, guardian, or trusted adult who can provide valuable support and advice.

What Is a Checking Account?

A checking account is like your financial command center. It's where you handle day-to-day transactions with convenience. You can deposit your money, write checks, withdraw cash, and make online payments seamlessly. These accounts are typically known for low-interest rates, but they provide you with quick access to your funds (FRANKENFIELD, 2018).

Setting up Your Checking Account

Getting a checking account is a breeze. You can apply online or visit a bank branch, and in no time, you'll have your checking account ready to use. You must provide basic personal information, like your Social Security number and identification.

Once you're set, you'll receive a debit card like a supercharged ATM card. You can use it to make purchases, withdraw cash, and more. You can also manage your account online, make transfers, and pay your bills from the comfort of your home (FRANKENFIELD, 2018).

Peace of Mind: FDIC Protection

Funds in a checking account at a bank are insured by the Federal Deposit Insurance Corp. (FDIC) for up to $250,000 per individual depositor per insured bank. That means your money is safe in case your bank encounters financial troubles. If you're opening an account at a credit union, you'll enjoy similar protection from the National Credit Union Association (FRANKENFIELD, 2018).

Different Strokes for Different Folks: Types of Checking Accounts

Checking accounts come in various flavors to suit different needs (FRANKENFIELD, 2018):

- **Commercial Checking Accounts:** These are for businesses with features tailored to their financial operations.
- **Student Checking Accounts:** Ideal for college students, they often offer perks like no maintenance or minimum balance fees while you're learning the ropes of money management.
- **Joint Checking Accounts:** This type allows two or more people, often spouses, to manage the account together. If you would like your parent to help you manage your funds, this would be a great way to start your financial journey.
- **Second Chance Accounts:** Designed for those who don't qualify for traditional checking accounts, they may have some restrictions and fees but can be a lifeline for rebuilding your financial standing.

How Banks Benefit From Checking Accounts

Banks make money from checking accounts through various fees. These accounts are also a way for banks to attract customers who may later consider taking out loans, mortgages, or certificates of deposit (CDs) from that bank.

Checking Accounts and Overdrafts

If you make a purchase that exceeds your checking account balance, your bank might cover the difference through overdraft protection, but it comes at a cost. For example, if your balance is

$50, and you make a $70 purchase, you can complete the transaction, but you might incur a $20 overdraft fee. To avoid overdraft charges, choose an account with no overdraft fees or set up balance alerts (FRANKENFIELD, 2018).

Checking Account Services

1. **Direct Deposit:** This convenient feature lets your employer deposit your paycheck electronically into your bank account. It ensures your funds are available immediately and can even score free checking at some banks (FRANKENFIELD, 2018).
2. **Wire Transfers:** These electronic money transfers securely move funds from one account to another.
3. **ATMs:** ATMs give you access to cash anytime, anywhere. Just be sure to understand your bank's fees for using out-of-network ATMs.
4. **Debit Cards:** These cards are your ticket to easy purchases. They work like credit cards but use the funds in your checking account. Many offer fraud protection, too.

Checking Accounts and Interest

Checking accounts usually don't offer high interest rates, if they offer any at all. However, some "high yield" checking accounts pay more than regular ones, but they may have specific requirements, such as maintaining a high balance or making many debit card transactions each month.

Checking Accounts and Credit Scores

Most basic checking account activities, like deposits and withdrawals, don't impact your credit score. Even closing a good-standing checking account won't affect your credit history.

Overdrafts on checking accounts only appear on your credit report if you fail to repay the overdraft.

Denied a Checking Account?

Banks and credit unions may review your checking account history before opening a new account. If you have a history of writing bad checks, unpaid overdraft fees, fraud, or if your account was closed for cause, you might be denied a new account. Federal law allows you to request a free checking account report annually from agencies like Certegy, ChexSystems, and others. If denied, consider second-chance checking accounts offered by many banks and credit unions (FRANKENFIELD, 2018).

Debit Card or Check Card?

Debit cards and check cards are the same thing. They allow you to make transactions using the funds in your checking account, and you can withdraw cash from ATMs.

Different Types of Checking Accounts

- Regular (Basic) Checking Accounts
- Premium Checking Accounts

- Student Checking Accounts
- Senior Checking Accounts
- Interest-Bearing Accounts
- Business Checking Accounts
- Rewards Checking Accounts

Checking Versus Savings Accounts

While a checking account is for frequent deposits and withdrawals, a savings account is designed for longer-term savings and typically offers higher interest rates. Checking accounts allows limitless withdrawals, whereas savings accounts usually limit the number of monthly transactions.

A checking account offers flexibility and FDIC protection, making it an ideal choice for short- term expenses. If you're considering opening one, compare account terms from different banks to understand their fees, benefits, and interest rates.

Now, you're all set to manage your money confidently using your checking account. Happy banking!

PROS AND CONS OF ONLINE BANKING

Online banking is the new kid on the financial block, causing quite a stir. You might have heard about it, but do you know the nitty-gritty details (George, 2021)?

Advantages: Why It's Awesome

Available Anywhere

Imagine you're a digital nomad or can't sit still in one place. Online banking has your back! You can manage your money from anywhere, whether on a beach, at grandma's house, or during math class (not that we endorse that last one).

All the Services You Love

Internet access = superpowers. You can pay bills, transfer cash, open accounts, check your balance, and even download monthly statements. The best part? No need to step into a physical bank; everything's a click away. You may also be able to save money by not getting a physical statement, and there's no need to shred it later, so someone doesn't have access to your account information.

Super-Easy Money Moves

Need to shuffle money from savings to checking on the fly? Online banking's got you covered. Even if you're chilling on a beach in Bali, you can set up a transfer in minutes. Are you helping out a college buddy? Easy-peasy-transfer money from your account to theirs.

No-Frills Banking

Remember those pesky fees at traditional banks? Online banks ditch most of them because they don't have fancy branches to maintain. Your wallet stays a little heavier!

Get More Bang for Your Buck

Online banks often offer better rates on savings accounts and certificates of deposit. That means more moolah for you, thanks to their lower operating costs.

Helpful Customer Service

Need a hand or have a burning question? Just give the customer service team a buzz. It's like having your own financial wizard hotline but without the wait (George, 2021).

Disadvantages: The Not-So-Cool Stuff

Tech Glitches = Panic Mode

Picture this: You're backpacking through Europe, and bam, you hit a "dead zone" with zero internet. Your online banking? Poof, gone until you find Wi-Fi. Yikes!

No Friendly Faces

You can stroll in, chat with a friendly bank officer at traditional banks, and grab a lollipop from the jar. Online banks? Not so much. It's all about faceless transactions.

You Don't Build Your Community

Local banks and credit unions are the cool cats of community building. They help their neighborhoods thrive. Online banks? Not so much. If you're all about local love, you might feel differently.

The Missing "Wet" Signature

Banks are more than money movers. They're the spot to get important documents notarized, requiring a "wet" signature. Online banks? Nope, they can't help you with that (George, 2021).

Is online banking the bee's knees or a bit of a buzzkill? It all depends on what you need. Online banking might be your jam if you're all about quick and easy banking. But stick with the traditional banks if you're looking for the whole shebang, from in-person signatures to safe deposit boxes.

Keep exploring your options, make informed choices, and remember, the financial world is your oyster.

PROTECT YOUR BANK ACCOUNT FROM FRAUDSTERS

So, you've got your bank account, and it's your treasure chest. But watch out because sneaky villains are trying to steal your hard-earned cash! Let's dive into the top five epic ways to protect your bank account from these cunning scammers (Patterson, 2020).

1. The Regular Account Check-up

Imagine your bank account is like a superhero HQ, and it's your job to keep it safe. Check it regularly, even if you don't use it every day. Set up monthly missions to balance your checking account. Make sure all those debits are legit. If something smells fishy, contact your bank's superhero squad pronto!

2. Shield Your PIN

Your Personal Identification Number (PIN) is like your bank account's secret handshake. Please don't give it to anyone, not even bank tellers. If a stranger calls asking for your PIN, hang up faster than a speeding bullet! Most banks have an automatic system connecting you to a real person without needing your PIN. Make sure your fellow sidekicks (family and friends) know the rule:

Never reveal your PIN! If you do, consider changing your PIN later to avoid someone using it to access your funds.

3. Craft an Invincible Password

Online banking is the new battleground for scammers. Protect your lair with a super-strong password. Don't be a sitting duck using obvious ones like your birthday or pet's name. Mix it up with a combo of numbers, letters, and symbols. A solid password will make it as tough as Thor's hammer for evildoers to crack!

4. Watch Your Back in Public Places

Sure, using your superpowers (smartphone) in coffee shops or fast-food joints with free Wi-Fi is tempting. But remember, these are public domains, and danger might be lurking. A hacker or a curious cat might sneak a peek at your banking secrets. For online banking missions, stick to the Bat Cave (your secure home network).

5. Beware of Sneaky ATMs

If you need cash, stick with the ATMs you know and trust, like your bank's Bat-Signal. Avoid ATMs in touristy spots or those that seem fishy. Not only will you dodge nasty ATM fees, but you'll also shield yourself from the sly tricks of scammers.

Remember, your bank account is your sidekick, and you're blazing your own trails. Protect it like the priceless gem it is, and you'll be ready to face any challenge that comes your way. Stay vigilant and keep your financial fortress secure!

When it comes to financial choices, it's okay to have your own Avengers team. A financial advisor is like Tony Stark, helping you build a solid financial suit. They can guide you to make the best decisions for your unique situation. So, embrace your financial superpowers and keep your money safe!

ACTIVITY: CHOOSING THE RIGHT BANK FOR YOU

If you're having a tough time deciding which bank to go with, check out this fantastic list of questions you can use to help you decide (Bennett, 2023).

1. Does the bank offer a variety of account options for you to choose from? For example: Checking, Savings, Money Market, and Credit Card accounts?
2. Are there any hidden costs involved? What about their service fees? What is their Overdraft Policy?
3. Is this bank popular in your neighborhood with easily accessible branches and ATMs for your convenience?
4. Is this bank Credit Union affiliated? What are their eligibility criteria?
5. Do the bank's features support your lifestyle? Do they offer high-yield savings, CD terms, separate savings accounts, and expense tracking?
6. Does the bank offer convenient digital features such as Mobile features, Card Locking, and Mobile banking alerts?
7. What are the terms and conditions (Account agreement details, Hidden fees, Service fee waiver options)?
8. Will your savings be federally insured (NCUA/FDIC insured)?
9. What promotional deals does the bank offer (Introductory rates, Terms of promotions)?

Once you've found the perfect bank, you can carefully start your journey toward financial freedom, one baby step at a time. In the next section, you will learn everything you need to know to optimize your savings and build a healthy bank balance.

PART II

UNDERSTANDING SAVINGS AND INVESTMENTS

5

THE ART OF SAVING

John Koon shattered age barriers by launching an auto parts business in New York City at just 16. His company, Extreme Performance Motorsports, became a major supplier for "Pimp My Ride," earning him millions.

Leveraging his connections, he co-founded a clothing company with rapper Young Jeezy, amassing a remarkable $40 million. John's story proves that age is no obstacle to achieving your dreams. Whether you're 16 or 60, with determination and passion, success is within reach. Keep pushing forward like John Koon, and make your dreams a reality (Costill, 2016).

Take heart if you're still working on that next big money-spinning idea. Your rise to success may not be as meteoric as John Koon's was. Still, I assure you that if you squirrel away as much of your funds as possible for as long as possible, you will also build your wealth, a dollar at a time. It starts with learning the art of saving.

YOU'RE NEVER TOO YOUNG TO START SAVING

If you're wondering why you should consider saving at such a young age, remember that the sooner you start, the more likely you will be to grow wealth. However, there are other compelling reasons to consider (Puharich, 2021).

1. **Financial Independence:** There's nothing quite like the freedom of having your own Money. Saving Money now means you won't have to rely on others to make decisions. Whether you want to go on a date, travel, or invest in your passions, having financial independence is a game-changer. It's your Money, and you can decide how to use it.
2. **Avoid Extra Work:** Isn't it nice to avoid working two jobs or taking night shifts to make ends meet? Early Money Saving can help you put less pressure on yourself when making work-related decisions. With less stress, your mind is more at ease, leading to increased creativity and productivity.
3. **Prepare for the Future:** As a teenager, you might not have many bills or responsibilities right now, but this phase won't last forever. It's important to start saving early to give yourself a head start on building wealth. By setting money aside now, you can avoid financial struggles and stress down the road. The financial habits you develop today can make your future more secure.
4. **Buy a Car:** Many teenagers aspire to own a car for the convenience, style, and fun of having their own wheels. However, cars are costly to purchase or maintain. Even if you plan to take out a loan, you'll likely need a down payment. Savings can help you reach that goal of buying a car, giving you the freedom to get around on your terms. Then, there are the added costs of car insurance and gas to

budget for when you become a car owner. Unfortunately, the younger you are, the higher the insurance costs because insurance is all about risk. New drivers with less experience present a higher risk. Insurance companies also factor in the type of car, the cost to replace it, the cost of replacement parts for repairs, and your average mileage... Sometimes, you could pay more for insurance than your actual car payments!

5. **Survival:** Life comes with necessities like food, shelter, clothing, and medical expenses. These costs can add up quickly. While your parents may be covering these expenses now, it's essential to understand that they won't do so indefinitely. By saving money early, you're preparing for the day when you'll need to take care of these essentials on your own.
6. **Money Management Skills:** Saving Money is a skill in itself. Learning the basics of money management can benefit various aspects of your life and career. Employers appreciate employees who can save money and are mindful of spending. Managing your finances wisely will reduce stress and provide a strong foundation for other areas of your life.
7. **College Debt Dodge:** College can be an exciting time filled with learning and personal growth opportunities. However, the financial burden of tuition and living expenses can be overwhelming. Add in student loans and credit card debt; your college years can be stressful. By saving early, you can graduate with less debt, giving you the freedom to focus on your education and having fun.
8. **Learn Financial Literacy:** There's no better way to learn financial literacy than by practicing it. Saving Money, budgeting, and investing are invaluable skills shaping your financial future. Starting early allows you to make and

learn from mistakes while they have a smaller impact. Your financial knowledge will grow alongside your bank account.

9. **Think About Retirement:** Believe it or not, it's never too early to think about retirement. The earlier you start saving, the more financial freedom you can enjoy later. Savings can allow you to retire earlier than you ever imagined. So, take into account the power of compound interest and the benefits of starting early.
10. **Less Debt, Less Stress:** A life without debt means paying less interest on loans. It's like saving Money within your savings. By avoiding unnecessary debt, you can decide when and how to take on loans, such as student loans, on your own terms. Not being buried in debt gives you peace of mind and financial stability.
11. **Investment Opportunities:** Saving Money doesn't just sit in a bank account; it can grow through investments. Legendary investor Warren Buffett began his investment journey when he was just 11 years old. While you may not be a teenager forever, your early savings could pave the way for a financially secure adulthood; it provides the opportunity to learn about investing hands-on.
12. **Take Control:** As a teenager, you're at a stage where you might be considering moving out, going on a trip, or even starting a business. With savings, you gain control over these decisions. You no longer depend on others to fund your dreams and aspirations. Savings allow you to take charge of your life and make choices that matter to you.
13. **Help Others:** Being able to lend a hand to those in need is incredibly fulfilling. Whether it's supporting your parents with bills or supporting a cause that is important to you, such as homelessness or animal shelters, having savings

allows you to be a source of support. Knowing you can make a difference in someone's life is a rewarding feeling.

Saving Money might seem challenging, but you can take plenty of small steps as a teen to start saving. Developing the right mindset, understanding the benefits, and putting money aside for the future are crucial to financial security and independence. By saving early, you're securing a brighter future where you're in control and financially empowered. So, start now, and watch your money grow!

THE IMPORTANCE OF AN EMERGENCY FUND

We get it; talking about Money isn't the most exciting thing in the world, especially when you'd rather daydream about the latest video game or that awesome party. But hold on, before you scroll away, what if we told you that understanding and planning your finances can be super cool and essential for your future adventures? No, really!

Let's dive into a topic that might not sound thrilling, but trust us, it's your secret weapon against life's unexpected curveballs: The Emergency Fund (Mydoh, 2023).

Emergency Fund: Your Financial Safety Net

You might wonder, "What's an emergency fund, and why should I care?" Well, picture it like this: It's your secret stash for those "uh-oh" moments in life. We're talking about a sudden car breakdown, a sick pet, or even a surprise dental bill. Trust us, you want to avoid being stuck in a financial pickle when these things pop up.

Why You Need It

Even as a teen, an emergency fund is like your financial buffer to get you out of a tight spot down the line. Here's the deal: Life can throw curveballs when you least expect it. Imagine losing a job, your beloved smartphone taking a dive into the pool, or facing an expensive root canal at the dentist. These aren't just everyday expenses; they're the kind that could put you in a tricky situation if you're not prepared.

And guess what? Parents can be the best superheroes, but they're not your personal emergency fund. Relying on them for every hiccup won't set you up for success. Instead, you could end up using credit cards or high-interest loans, and that's like digging a financial hole you'll have to climb out of. Besides, everyone knows that when you owe your folks money, it often comes with some strings attached, right? The best feeling in the world is knowing that you built your success story from the ground up on the merits of your own efforts.

Remember, Emergency Funds Are for Emergencies!

Now, we know how tempting it is to consider a fabulous vacation, new clothes, or adopting a pet as "emergencies," but they're not. Emergency funds are there for real, unexpected, and necessary situations. Parties, holidays, or wardrobe upgrades are different deals altogether, and you should plan separately for them.

So, How Much Should You Save?

The big question: "How much should I have in my emergency fund?" There's no one-size-fits-all answer, but a general rule is to aim for three to six months' worth of essential living expenses.

That's stuff like rent, bills, groceries–the things you need to keep the lights on.

The actual dollar amount varies depending on where you live and your unique situation. If saving a lot seems overwhelming, start small. Even a couple of hundred dollars tucked away is better than nothing.

How to Build Your Emergency Fund

Building your emergency fund doesn't have to be a daunting task. Here's how to get started:

1. **Determine How Much You Need:** List all your essential expenses, like your phone, food, transportation, and any potential medical or dental costs. Add them up for one month, then multiply that by the number of months you're aiming for. Voila, you've got a goal!
2. **Budget Smart:** Look at your monthly income and determine how much you can save for your emergency fund. It's all about balance, so plan according to your income, expenses, and savings goals.
3. **Create a Separate Savings Account:** Keep your emergency fund separate from your regular spending. Choose an account with no withdrawal fees and one earning a little interest. Automate your savings so that a portion of your income goes directly into this account. It's like magic!
4. **Track Your Spending:** To save more, keep an eye on where your money goes. Small things like cutting back on takeout or limiting in-app purchases can help you save extra bucks.

And here's the fun part: Think of creative ways to make saving a game. Challenge yourself, compete with friends, and reward your progress. Who doesn't love a gold star for financial success?

In a Nutshell

An emergency fund is your secret weapon against unexpected twists and turns. It's not about being a downer; it's about being smart and prepared for whatever comes your way. Saving now means you don't have to stress about money when you need it the most.

So, start building your emergency fund today. Your future self will thank you for it. And who knows, once you've mastered the art of saving, you can effortlessly save up for those great adventures and fun stuff, too!

UNLOCKING THE MOOLAH: HOW TO STACK YOUR CASH

Hey there, future money-making moguls! So, you're looking to rake in some cash but still rocking those teen vibes? Don't worry; you're in the right place! Here's the lowdown on how to score some serious dough and start your journey toward financial freedom (*Ultimate Guide: How to Earn Money as a Teenager*, n.d.).

Sweet Gigs for Teens

Let's talk gigs, not that kinda gig, but ways for you to make bank while keeping those study sessions on your radar (*Ultimate Guide: How to Earn Money as a Teenager*, n.d.).

Retail Extravaganza

Retail is your ticket to learning customer service, being responsible, and making friends with coworkers. Plus, you might snag some epic employee discounts. Perks, anyone?

Café Connoisseur

Are you an early riser? The aroma of fresh pastries and that morning coffee buzz may be your jam. Working in a café or bakery, you can pocket hourly wages plus those sweet tips.

Restaurant Hustle

Restaurants offer fast-paced action, and you can jump into various roles, from bussing tables to food running. Plus, it's like a training ground for life skills; you'll be a pro multitasker in no time!

Family Biz Star

If your family owns a business, diving in is your golden opportunity. You'll make money while bonding with the family and learning the ropes of the trade.

Nailing the Job Hunt

Don't freak out; feeling intimidated when hunting for your first gig is totally normal. Here's your game plan (*Ultimate Guide: How to Earn Money as a Teenager*, n.d.):

Resume Remix

Create a stellar resume even if you haven't worked a day in your life. List your skills, languages you speak, and any helpful experiences, like volunteering or contributing to bake sales.

Understand the Legal Deets

Depending on where you live, some jobs require special paperwork for minors. Your school's guidance counselor is an excellent start for assistance.

Know Your Rights

Teens have some specific job protections. You usually can't work under 14 (with exceptions), and there are hourly limits if you're under 16. Check labor laws and know your rights!

Minimum Wage Magic

As a teen, you might be looking at a lower minimum wage when you start, but it can increase after 90 days. Stay sharp; you can chat about your pay with your fellow workers.

Tax Talk

Once you're rolling in the dough (more than $12,550 annually), you'll be besties with tax forms.

Cash Flow Without a Job

Don't have a formal job? No worries, there are still ways to cash in (*Ultimate Guide: How to Earn Money as a Teenager*, n.d.):

1. **Tutoring Talents:** Share your wisdom and tutor others in academics, sports, or music. You can make some serious green.
2. **Errands and Chores:** Help neighbors and family friends with errands and chores. Grocery shopping, yard work, and fixer skills are your golden ticket.
3. **Babysitting Boss:** Babysitting is a classic gig. It's often well-paying, and parents might even throw in some tips.
4. **Sell Your Stuff:** If you've got clothes or random goodies lying around, sell them online. There are loads of platforms: Depop, Poshmark, Vinted, and more.
5. **Crafting Cash:** If you're crafty, open an Etsy shop, or go for Amazon Handmade and start selling your handcrafted goodies.
6. **Survey Hustle:** Share your thoughts and earn some moolah with paid surveys on platforms like Swagbucks and Survey Junkie.
7. **Game On:** If you're into gaming, you can stream on Twitch or use apps like Mistplay, Gamehag, and Drop to cash in on your gaming skills.
8. **Content Creator:** Start a podcast, TikTok, or YouTube channel. You can monetize through affiliate marketing, traditional marketing, or Patreon as you gain followers.
9. **App-Based Income (for 18+):** Once you hit 18, explore apps like TaskRabbit, Jobble, and Upwork for odd jobs. For pet lovers, Wag! and Rover are paw-some options. And if you've got wheels, give food delivery a spin with DoorDash, UberEats, Grubhub, and Postmates.

Super Savvy

Remember to save when you've got the green rolling in! Set financial goals, create savings buckets, and watch your money grow.

Save for that dream guitar, gaming console, or extraordinary adventure: it's never too early to start building your financial future.

Your parents can help too. They might match the Money you save, helping you learn about banking, budgeting, and investing. And remember those birthday and holiday gifts; they can be a sweet addition to your savings.

That's it, future finance pros! With the right strategies, you can stack that cash, save smart, and start your money journey early. Get out there and chase those dollar bills; your financial future starts now!

TYPES OF SAVINGS ACCOUNTS

You might discover that managing your Money can be a bit of a maze, but fear not because we're here to break down six types of savings accounts just for you. So let's dive in and make sense of your options (CEPF, n.d.):

1. High-Yield Savings Accounts

Best for: People who are like banking digitally

Interest rates: High

Pros: High interest rates, low fees, low opening deposits

Cons: No bank branches

High-yield savings accounts are your go-to if you're about the digital world. These accounts are usually with online banks, which means no actual bank buildings but loads of great benefits.

They offer high-interest rates, which means more money in your pocket. Most of these accounts don't have annoying monthly fees, and you don't need much cash to get started; some even let you open an account with no initial deposit!

2. Money Market Accounts

Best for: Those who want to easily access their savings

Interest rates: Usually high

Benefits: Elevated interest rates, provision of debit cards or paper checks.

Drawbacks: Higher initial deposits and limitations on the number of transactions through electronic transfer, check, or debit card.

Money market accounts closely resemble savings accounts, available online and in traditional banks, with online options typically presenting more attractive offers. These accounts provide substantial interest rates, and some even include features like debit cards or paper checks, enhancing the accessibility of your funds. The initial deposit required for these accounts might be slightly higher than that of regular savings accounts.

3. Cash Management Accounts

Ideal for: Individuals seeking an all-in-one banking and investment solution

Interest Rates: Moderate

Advantages: Above-average rates, minimal fees, unrestricted withdrawals

Disadvantages: Rates are lower than High-Yield Savings (HYS) accounts, and physical branches are absent.

Cash management accounts offer a fusion of checking and savings functionalities. Online banking platforms commonly provide these accounts, offering considerable flexibility. Some even boast interest rates comparable to those of high-yield savings accounts. These accounts streamline your financial activity by accommodating spending, saving, and investing within a single platform, albeit without physical branches.

Pros: High interest rates, debit cards or paper checks

Cons: Higher opening deposits and a limited number of transactions you can make by check, debit card, or electronic transfer.

Money market accounts are similar to savings accounts. You can find them online or in physical banks, but the online ones often have the best deals. They offer high interest rates, plus some throw in a debit card or paper checks, making your Money super accessible. They might ask for more cash to start your account than regular savings accounts.

4. **Certificates of Deposits (CDs)**

Best for: People who can tuck away Money for a long time

Interest rates: Usually high

Pros: Higher rates with longer terms, fixed rates, no monthly fees

Cons: Lower rates with shorter terms, higher opening deposits, penalties for withdrawing money early

CDs are like the secret vault of savings. You lock your Money in for a set period—it could be a few months or several years—and in return, you get super high-interest rates. These rates stay fixed, so you know exactly what you're earning. CDs are available at physical and online banks, but the online ones usually offer better rates. Good news: You shouldn't have to pay monthly service fees.

5. Traditional Savings Accounts

Best for: People who like banking in person

Interest rates: Low

Pros: Access to a bank branch

Cons: Low-interest rates, high monthly fees

Traditional savings accounts are your old-school options. You can walk into a bank or credit union to open one. They're perfect if you love that face-to-face banking vibe. However, they usually offer lower interest rates. They might hit you with monthly fees, though you might be able to dodge them. But the benefit? You can chat with a real-life banker when you have questions.

6. Specialty Savings Accounts

Best for: People with specific or unique savings goals

Interest rates: Varies by account type

Pros: Save for a particular goal

Cons: Only for certain kinds of people; some restrictions on withdrawals

If you have unique goals, specialty savings accounts are the way to go. These accounts cater to specific purposes. For example, health savings accounts help you save for medical expenses in the future, and kids' savings accounts are designed for minors to learn about saving. Be sure to check if you qualify and if there are any rules about when you can take your Money out.

So there you have it, teens, the six savings account options waiting for you to make your money moves. The key is to pick the one that matches your goals and lifestyle. Happy saving!

ACTIVITY

Saving Money isn't just about stashing cash away; it's also about achieving your goals and dreams. So, let's get interactive!

Grab your phone or a notebook, or use your noggin to answer these questions.

Describe One or Two Things You'd Like to Have but Can't Afford Right Now.

It could be the latest gaming console, a sweet set of wheels (aka your first car), or moving into your own place. Whatever it is, jot it down!

Why Are These Things Worth Saving For?

Think about why these dreams are important to you. Is it because they'd make you happy, help you level up, or bring your passions to life? Share your thoughts!

How Will Having These Things Make Your Life Better?

Imagine having these things in your life. How would they change your daily routine or long-term plans? Share the ways they'd make your life epic!

Feel free to chat with your pals and family, or even talk to yourself (we all do it, don't worry) about these dreams. Once you've got your answers, you'll have a crystal-clear picture of what's worth saving for. And remember, you're one step closer to turning those dreams into reality!

To recap, you have your strong hustle going, saving for something special and edging closer to turning your dreams into a reality. If you are super-smart about it, you can grow your wealth quickly by learning how to use the unique opportunities offered by intelligent investing and banking. This brings us to the section on Compounding and how you can make it work for you.

6

COMPOUNDING WIZARDRY

In the world of teenage creativity, Emily Matson and Julianne Goldmark launched Emi-Jay in seventh grade. They adored TV show hair accessories but found them too pricey and complicated. Their solution? A trip to LA's garment district for materials.

What began as a hobby exploded when Jennifer Aniston flaunted their hair tie on the red carpet. They named their project Emi-Jay, created a website, and voilà, a business was born. Their trendy products are now sold in over 3,000 North American specialty stores worldwide. Celebs like Jennifer Aniston, Gigi Hadid, and Kim Kardashian are fans.

Emi-Jay didn't stop at hair ties; they've partnered with brands like Revolve, Juicy Couture, and Summer Fridays. Take a lesson from Emily and Julianne; they turned a simple idea into an international success, and you can too (How to Become a Teenage Millionaire: 15 Success Stories, 2018)!

So, What's This Compound Interest Thing?

Simply put, it's when you save a bit of money, and it magically multiplies over time, thanks to some smart investing. Imagine planting a tiny seed that grows into a massive tree but with cash.

How Does It Work?

When you save some money, the magic happens. Your earnings get reinvested, and they start earning money themselves. It's like money making more money. And this keeps happening year after year, growing your savings exponentially.

GET A HEAD START FOR MAXIMUM IMPACT

Saving money might not seem like the most exciting thing in the world, but what if we told you there's a secret formula to making your money grow? It's called "compound interest," and it's like a low-effort tool that can totally change your financial game (Field, 2021).

Why You Need to Get on This Train Right Now

Starting early with your savings is like building your skills or becoming a pro at something. Think about how famous chefs don't become culinary stars overnight. They spend years honing their craft. It's a bit like compound interest. You put in a little effort now; later on, you won't have to stress about money.

The earlier you start, the more time your money has to work its magic. For example, if a 25-year- old starts investing $200 per month with a six percent return, they could have nearly $400,000 by age 65. But if they wait until 35 to start, they'd have only about half of that. So, the sooner you start, the better!

The Power of Starting Early: Scenario Time

Imagine a 20-year-old, Sarah, who invests $1,000 today. If she doesn't touch it until she's 70, she could end up with around $32,000. But if she waits until 30, she'd only have about $16,000. And if she puts it off until she's 40, she'd be looking at just $8,000.

Starting at 20 and contributing $1,000 annually could grow her savings to a whopping $465,000 by the time she's 70. Beginning at 30 would mean she'd have around $225,000; at 40, it'd be about $105,000.

Compound Interest Scenario

Now, let's check out two friends, Carolina and Andy. Carolina starts saving at 25 and stops at 44. Andy begins at 45 and ends at 64, each saving the same amount with a six percent annual return.

Carolina, who starts early, ends up with a massive $110,000 more than Andy when they reach 65. Carolina's money enjoys up to 40 years of growth, while Andy only gets 20 years. So, if Carolina keeps saving until she reaches 65, she'd have around $243,000.

The lesson here? Time is your best friend with compound interest. The sooner you start saving and investing, the more time you have to make the magic happen. It's like free money that you want to take advantage of.

So, start early, save a little, and let your money grow over time. It's like planting the seeds of your financial future, and trust us, you'll thank yourself later.

COMPOUND GROWTH ON INVESTMENTS AND INTEREST

Ready to discover the incredible world of compounding and how it can make your cash grow? Let's break it down without all the fancy jargon (*What Is Compound Growth - Wells Fargo,* n.d.).

How It Works

Imagine you tossing $1,000 into an investment that gives you a six percent return. You'd make $60 in year one, turning your total to $1,060. Now, here's where it gets exciting. In year two, you're not just earning six percent on your original $1,000 but on the full $1,060. So you make $63.60 and now have $1,123.60.

The Magic of Time

The longer you let your money do its thing, the more it multiplies. In our example, after 30 years, you'd make a whopping $325.10 each year! That's more than five times your first-year earnings. Check out the Time Value of Money (TMV) section in Chapter One.

Pro Tip:

To make compounding work like a charm, reinvest your earnings automatically. Patience is key. Don't cash out the moment you see those dollars pile up. If you're using a taxable account, remember that you'll pay some taxes on the interest, dividends, and capital gains, even if you reinvest.

Want to supercharge your money growth? Add extra cash to your account regularly. Ask your bank or employer about automatic transfers. The more money you put in, the faster your wealth can grow.

Compounding is like a money-making machine. Start early, save, invest, and watch your cash grow while you chill.

Stay wise with your finances, and remember, it's never too early to build your wealth.

THE RULE OF 72

Wanna learn a secret formula to grow your cha-ching? The "Rule of 72" is your ticket to Easy Street (Leavitt, 2023).

So, What's the Rule of 72?

It's a simple way to figure out how long it'll take for your money to double at a specific interest rate. In other words, how long before your cash multiplies? Think of it like leveling up your money in a game.

The Math Behind It

Say you have $1,000 saved up, and you're earning a four percent interest rate (which is like the bonus points for your money). To determine how long it'll take for your $1,000 to become $2,000, divide 72 by your interest rate. Here's the math: 72/4 = 18. So, in 18 years, your $1,000 becomes $2,000. Cool, right?

But here's the deal: The Rule of 72 isn't perfect. It works best when your interest rate is between 5% and 12%. If it's higher or lower, it's less accurate. But it's still a handy tool to get a rough idea of how your money can grow.

More Math, Less Boring Stuff

Now, the Rule of 72 is all about compounding interest. That's when your money makes money on the money it's already made, like a snowball getting bigger as it rolls downhill. And it's your patience that makes it work. Don't touch that money until it doubles!

But there's a twist: if you're dealing with inflation (when stuff gets more expensive over time), you can use the Rule of 72 to see how long it takes for your money's buying power to get cut in half. Let's say inflation is at eight percent. Then, 72 divided by 8 equals 9. So, in nine years, your money's purchasing power is halved.

Why Should You Care?

Here's the cool part: The Rule of 72 can help you plan your financial future. Suppose you're saving for something big, like an apartment, college, or business venture. In that case, knowing how your money can grow over time is a game-changer. It helps you make smart choices, like how much to invest and when to start.

So, if you want your money to grow, remember the Rule of 72. It's your secret weapon for making your money work hard for you. And the best part? You can start using it right now!

Stay smart with your cash and quickly level up your financial game.

ACTIVITY

Using the Compound Interest Calculator

Try giving the online compound interest calculator a whirl. This is a powerful tool to help you understand how your savings and investments can grow over time. Let's break down how to use this tool (The Calculator site, 2019).

How to Calculate Compound Interest

Here's how to use the calculator:

- **Initial Investment (Principal Amount):** Enter how much money you're starting with.
- **Interest Rate:** Tell us the percentage of interest you'll earn each year. For example, if it's five percent, enter five.
- **Compound Frequency:** How often is your interest calculated and added to your savings. If it's annually, choose '1'. If it's monthly, select '12'.
- **Time:** This is how long you plan to save or invest. Enter the number of years.
- **Regular Deposits or Withdrawals:** You can include those here if you're adding money regularly or taking some out.

Why Is Compound Interest So Important?

Warren Buffett, one of the world's wealthiest investors, says it's a big part of how he made his wealth. It's a superpower for growing your money!

Calculating Monthly Compound Interest

If your interest is calculated monthly, use this formula:

A = P (1 + r/12) ^ (12t)

- **A:** Your future balance
- **P:** Initial balance
- **r:** Annual interest rate
- **t:** Time in years

The Benefits of Compound Interest

Here's where it gets exciting. The more often your interest is compounded, the faster your money grows. It's like a snowball effect on your savings. Check out this graph to see it in action!

How Much Will You Have in the Future?

Imagine you start with $10,000 in a savings account, earning five percent interest per year, with interest compounded yearly. Here's how it has grown over 20 years:

- **Year 1:** $10,000 + $500 interest = $10,500
- **Year 2:** $10,500 + $525 interest = $11,025
- **Year 3:** $11,025 + $551.25 interest = $11,576.25

And so on... After 20 years, you'll have $26,532.98. That's a total interest of $16,532.98; your initial $10,000 has grown by 165%!

Compound Interest With Regular Deposits

If you add extra money regularly, like $100 monthly, your balance after 20 years could reach $67,121. The interest on your $34,000 deposits would be $33,121. That's the power of saving and investing over time!

Where to Invest for Compound Interest

This calculator helps you see how your money can grow, but we can't tell you exactly where to invest. It's a personal choice. We recommend talking to a financial advisor who can consider your situation.

Frequently Asked Questions

When is my interest compounded?

You can choose whether it's at the start or end of each period.

Can I include regular withdrawals?

Yes, you can include them in your calculations.

What is the effective annual interest rate?

It's the rate you actually earn on your money after compounding.

What is RoR/TWR?

RoR is the return on your investment, while TWR accounts for deposits and withdrawals.

By now, you would have learned that the trick to growing your money is to start early and make wise decisions about your spending-saving dynamic. You are getting ready to start raking in some serious cash in a few years.

In the next chapter, we take a peek into the world of investing, which, although risky, can have its own rewards.

Powerful Inspiration from Ollie

> *"Be bold enough to use your voice, brave enough to listen to your heart, and strong enough to live the life you have always imagined."*
>
> — *ANONYMOUS*

Remember Ollie Forsyth, the boy I told you about in the introduction? His own business and $5,000 payout within the first few months is inspiration enough when you're thinking about how powerful it is to take charge of your finances from a young age, but it's his later venture, The Budding Entrepreneur Club, that I want to talk about right now.

Ollie set this venture up to give more young people the opportunity to succeed. He recognized the potential out there for teenagers, and he knew that if they were going to make it, they needed more than they'd be able to get from their school books.

In fact, it's precisely because of this that you're here reading this now. Financial education is the one piece of the puzzle missing from the school system, and the reason three-quarters of teenagers need more confidence in their knowledge of personal finance is a side-effect of this.

When you understand how money works (and how to make it work for you), your future becomes so much easier to navigate ... and so does your present! And a world in which more people understand their finances is definitely a world you want to live in. So, I'd like you to take a moment to follow in Olly's footsteps and help open this door to more young people. The best part is you don't have to set up a whole network like he did—all you need to do is write a few sentences!

By leaving a review of this book on Amazon, you'll help other teenagers find this crucial information and show them just how important financial literacy is.

Reviews are how people find resources, and writing one is an easy way to contribute to this important network of young people who want to succeed.

Thank you for your help with this. It might not seem like much, but your contribution makes a huge difference.

Scan the QR code below

7

FUNDAMENTALS OF INVESTING

FRASER DOHERTY'S SUPERJAM: A TEEN'S SWEET SUCCESS

Meet Fraser Doherty, a Scottish teen who turned his grandmother's jam recipes into a million-dollar dream. At 14, Fraser began making jams from these cherished recipes for family and friends at his local church. The response was overwhelming, and his homemade jams quickly became a hit (How to Become a Teenage Millionaire: 15 Success Stories, 2018).

By age 16, Fraser's jam-making business was booming. His SuperJam found its way into 184 Waitrose stores, 300 Tesco outlets, and even international giant Walmart.

The secret to his success? Fraser's unwavering passion. He constantly tweaked his recipes, moved production from his parents' kitchen to a rented factory, and borrowed $9,000 for experimentation. However, money was not his driving force. His motto? "I can't be preoccupied with money; I make jam because it's what I love to do."

Fraser's journey from a teen with a family recipe to a jam-making sensation is an inspiring example of what can be achieved at any age with dedication and passion. His story reminds us that dreams can come true, one jar of jam at a time. So, the next time you savor SuperJam, remember it's not just a condiment; it's a taste of sweet success crafted by a passionate teen entrepreneur.

TYPES OF INVESTMENTS: STOCKS, BONDS, AND MORE

You are never too young to start on your investment journey. The fundamental types of investment options currently available are mentioned briefly here in the hopes that you will go ahead and research the ones that appeal to you in greater detail as your interest in investments grows (Geier, 2021).

- **Stocks:** Imagine owning a piece of your favorite company, like Apple or Microsoft. When their value goes up, your money does, too. But be ready for the rollercoaster ride – stocks can also go down.
- **Bonds:** Think of bonds as loaning money to a company or government. In return, they pay you interest. Safe, but not as thrilling as stocks.
- **Mutual Funds:** It's like joining a money club with other people. Pros make the decisions about which stocks or bonds to buy. Easy for newbies!
- **Exchange-Traded Funds (ETFs):** These are like mutual funds but traded on the stock market. They can be super diversified and easy to buy or sell. 'Diversified' means spreading your money into lots of different things instead of putting it all in one place. It's like not putting all your eggs in one basket. So, when we talk about diversified Exchange-Traded Funds (ETFs), these are investments that include a mix of many different things, like stocks from

different companies or bonds from other sources. Because you're spreading your money, it can help reduce the risk. If one company or investment doesn't do well, it's okay because you have other things in your ETF that might be doing better. It's like playing it safe by not putting all your money in one place.

- **Certificates of Deposit (CDs):** You lend money to a bank for a set time and get paid interest when it's over, like a super safe savings account.
- **Retirement Plans:** These are like special accounts where you save for retirement while getting tax benefits. Your money is invested in stuff like stocks and bonds.
- **Options:** These are like bets on whether a stock will go up or down. They can be tricky, so approach them with caution.
- **Annuities:** An annuity is like a savings plan where you pay in and, in the future, get paid back periodically; an excellent way to guarantee some income when you're older.
- **Derivatives:** These are pretty advanced; they're like contracts based on the price of something else, and you can make or lose big bucks.
- **Commodities:** Investing in physical things like gold, oil, or even pork bellies (yes, that's a thing). The prices can be wild!
- **Hybrid Investments:** These mix stocks and bonds. Preferred shares are like stocks with benefits; convertible bonds can become stocks. Fancy!

So, how do you get into this investing game? You've got two options:

1. **Online Brokerage Account:** You're the boss. You open an account and buy and sell stuff on your own. Freedom!
2. **Hire a Financial Advisor:** If you prefer someone to help you, hire a financial advisor. They'll make decisions for you based on your goals.

Remember, each type of investment comes with its risks and rewards. So, be smart and pick the one that suits your goals. Investing is about growing your money, but it's like a game; there are no guarantees. Start small, learn, and grow. Who knows, you might turn into a teenage investing genius!

The True Cost of Investing

Are you thinking about starting your investment journey? It's an exciting prospect, but before you dive in, some important things must be considered. One crucial factor is understanding the actual cost of investing. This means being aware of the fees associated with different investment accounts and, just as importantly, the cost of not doing your homework.

1. Account Fees: The Price of Participation

Investment accounts come in various shapes and sizes. Some may charge you a fee every time you make a trade, while others offer their services for free. It's important to know what you're signing up for. Think of these fees as the price of admission to the world of investing. Each trade or monthly fee can add up over time, potentially affecting your overall returns. Before choosing an account, make sure you understand their fee structure.

2. Financial Advisors: A Valuable but Costly Resource

Many people seek guidance from financial advisors, and they can provide valuable insights. However, financial advisors also come with their costs. They might charge fees or take a percentage of your investments. So, when considering a financial advisor, doing your homework is crucial. Research their background, reputation, and fees to ensure they fit your financial goals well.

3. The Price of Ignorance

Learning from your mistakes is valid, but the cost of ignorance can be high when investing. Suppose you put your money into an investment without understanding it, and it loses value. In that case, that money may be gone forever. Investing with a solid company means you will cement your loss if you sell when the market is down. However, if you have done your research and the company is stable enough to weather a little market turbulence, stay the course. You may incur additional fees when you sell that investment and buy another. This cycle of loss and costs can quickly erode your savings.

4. The Power of Research

Before putting a significant amount of money into investments, it's essential to do your research. Fortunately, numerous free resources are available, from online articles and videos to books on investing. Learning the basics can help you make more informed decisions and avoid costly mistakes.

Investing doesn't have to be a gamble. Learning through experience is okay, but it's better to arm yourself with knowledge before you start. Research is your friend, and it can help you understand the risks and rewards of investing. So, take the time to learn and explore your options. Make informed choices to reduce the cost of investing and increase your chances of financial success.

CRYPTOCURRENCIES

Let's dive into the world of cryptocurrency, or as we like to call it, digital moolah (Kaspersky, 2022).

What's Cryptocurrency?

Think of it as digital money, but not the kind you can hold in your hand. It's all virtual and super high-tech. Cryptocurrencies use cryptography to keep your transactions secure; no banks, no paper bills, just pure digital magic.

How Does It Work?

Cryptocurrencies run on something called a blockchain. It's like a super-secure digital ledger that records every transaction. Imagine it as a giant online piggy bank where everyone can see the transactions, but no one can touch your coins without your secret keys.

Buying Cryptocurrency

So, do you want to dive into the world of digital riches? First, you need to choose a platform to buy and trade cryptocurrencies. You've got two options:

1. **Traditional brokers:** They handle crypto, stocks, and stuff. They are less crypto-focused but have lower fees.
2. **Cryptocurrency exchanges:** These platforms are all about digital coins. More crypto choices, but they might charge

higher fees.

Once you've picked a platform, you fund your account using real money (like dollars or euros). You can even use a credit card or bank transfer. Be cautious with credit cards, though some don't like crypto transactions.

What Can You Buy?

Lots of things! Tech gadgets, luxury stuff, and even cars. Some companies, like Microsoft, AT&T, and even luxury watch sellers, accept cryptocurrency as payment. It's like buying your favorite things with digital gold.

But remember, the crypto world is like a rollercoaster. Prices can go up and down like crazy. So, be careful and don't invest your lunch money.

Storing Your Coins

You don't just leave your digital treasures lying around, right? It would help to have a crypto wallet and a digital safe to keep your secret keys. There are hot wallets (online) and cold wallets (offline). Hot wallets are like digital pockets, while cold wallets are super secure, like a bank vault.

Stay Safe

The crypto world is full of opportunities but also risks. Scammers love it, so be cautious. Watch out for fake websites, crazy promises of guaranteed profits, and people pretending to be celebs. If it sounds too good to be true, it probably is.

Also, ensure a good antivirus protects your digital coins from cyber villains.

Bottom Line

Cryptocurrency is the future of money, but it's also a wild and risky world. If you want in, do your homework, diversify your investments, and be ready for a rollercoaster ride. And most importantly, don't invest what you can't afford to lose.

PEER-TO-PEER LENDING

Imagine you need some cash but want to avoid going through a bank. P2P lending is like asking a buddy for a loan, but your buddies are people you've never met online (Kagan, 2020). It's like getting a little help from the internet community!

Cutting Out the Middleman

In P2P lending, you don't deal with banks or financial institutions. Nope, it's just you and another person making a financial deal. No middleman, no fuss.

Also Known As...

You might hear P2P lending called "social lending" or "crowd lending." It's like you're borrowing money from a virtual crowd of helpful folks.

How It Works

P2P lending websites connect people who need money with those who want to lend it. These websites set the interest rates and terms, making the process smooth.

Here's how it rolls:

- You, the lender, create an account and put some cash into it.
- Folks who need money post profiles that tell potential lenders their financial story.
- You can check out these profiles, pick one that tickles your fancy, and lend money.
- The website manages all the money transfers and monthly payments. It's like having a super-intelligent money robot as your assistant.

History Lesson

P2P lending didn't even exist before 2005! It was like a financial superhero that suddenly appeared. It started as a way for folks who didn't fit into traditional banking systems to get loans, like students and small business owners.

But Wait, There's More!

Nowadays, P2P lending has evolved. You can use it to pay off pesky credit card debt or finance home improvements or cars. If your credit score is in tip-top shape, you might even score a loan with lower interest rates than the big banks offer.

Risks and Rewards

But hold up! P2P lending isn't all rainbows and unicorns. Sometimes, folks who borrow money don't pay it back. The default risk is higher than traditional banks, so keep that in mind.

It's like a fun but somewhat risky adventure. Remember to check the fees and commissions, too. Like traditional banks, P2P websites might hit you with loan origination fees, late fees, and other charges.

Is P2P Lending Safe?

P2P lending is a bit riskier than stashing your cash in a savings account, but the interest rates can be sweeter than a candy store. Since you're lending directly to people, you take on the risk banks usually carry.

How Big Is This Thing?

P2P lending is huge! In 2022, it was worth over $134 billion, and it's predicted to grow even bigger by 2030. People are loving it!

How Can You Join the P2P Lending Fun?

Joining P2P lending is easy. Create an account on a P2P lending site, and you can start lending money to folks in need. Depending on how much risk you're comfortable with, you can even choose your borrowers. Some P2P lending sites are public companies, so you can invest in them by buying their stock.

The Lowdown

P2P lending is all about helping each other out, and it's pretty amazing. But remember, with great power (and rewards) comes great responsibility (and risks). Make sure you understand the fees and the chances of loans not getting paid back.

So, if you're thinking about P2P lending, read the fine print, be a smart lender, and make a little extra cash while helping others. It's like being a financial superhero of the internet!

RISK AND REWARD: UNDERSTANDING INVESTMENT DYNAMICS

Investing is like embarking on a grand adventure full of excitement and challenges. It's not just about multiplying your money; it's about skillfully navigating the intricate dance of risk and reward to make the most of your financial journey. So, let's break it down step by step (O Niell, 2023):

Understanding Risk and Reward

At its core, investing is a delicate balance between two key players: risk and reward. Think of it as a complex game; the higher your risk, the greater the potential reward and the higher the chance of stumbling. To play the game right, you need to master the art of understanding this delicate relationship.

The Different Faces of Risk

Risk is like hidden traps and challenges in a game; you never know what's coming. It's possible to face undesirable outcomes or financial losses in your investments. Risks can come from various sources: changes in interest rates, the ever-shifting economic landscape, unpredictable market fluctuations, and the performance of individual companies.

To be a successful player, you must be aware of these lurking risks. Like a seasoned gamer, you should also diversify your Investments across various assets, spreading your bets to minimize the impact of a single risky move. This diversification acts as your shield, protecting your portfolio from significant losses and ensuring you stay in the game.

The Glorious Reward

Ah, the reward; it's like conquering the final boss in a game and reaping the treasures. In the world of finance, it's the return or profit you gain from your investments. This could mean your investments increase in value, receiving those sweet dividend payouts or interest payments.

Rewards are like the trophy of your investing journey, the reason you took on the risks in the first place. And here's the catch: The potential reward often lures us into the game. The higher the risk, the greater the possible reward and the heightened chance of facing obstacles.

What Makes Risk and Reward Dance

These two, risk and reward, are like dance partners who never leave each other's side. In investments, higher risks tend to be linked with higher potential rewards. Still, they also bring the specter of more considerable losses. Conversely, lower-risk investments are more like a safety net, offering lower returns but a smoother journey with fewer pitfalls.

Balancing risk and reward is like choosing a game's difficulty level. It's about understanding your risk tolerance, the time you can commit, and your ultimate financial objectives. In this game, everyone plays by their rules.

A Few Game-Changing Factors

Let's delve deeper into the elements that affect risk and reward:

- **Market Fluctuations:** As an unexpected plot twist can change your game strategy, market fluctuations can shake up your investments. These fluctuations can be triggered by economic conditions, political events, or real-life events (like natural disasters). To stay ahead, you must keep an eye on market trends and economic indicators and make well-informed decisions.

- **Investment Types:** Different investments are like game characters with their own skills and risks. Stocks are the daring knights—risky but potentially high reward, while bonds are like the wise sages—lower risk, lower rewards. And then you have the mages of the group, mixing growth and income, offering a bit of both.
- **Time Horizon:** Your time horizon is like choosing the duration of a game quest. The longer you can commit, the more adaptable you become to market ups and downs. But if your journey is short and sweet, you might want to stick to lower-risk investments to avoid big hiccups.

Risk Tolerance and Your Quest

Now, let's talk about risk tolerance, which is like choosing your character's class in a game. It's all about your ability to handle investments' ups and downs. To gauge your risk tolerance, consider your emotional reactions to financial rollercoasters, the time you can dedicate, and your overall financial situation.

The Quest Objectives

Every game has objectives, right? In the investment game, you set your goals, and these can fall into four categories:

- **Income:** This is like choosing to be the resourceful rogue, focused on generating regular income through interests and dividends. It's for those who prefer a more conservative, stable approach.

- **Growth and Income:** Consider yourself a versatile warrior seeking growth and regular income. This approach is for those comfortable with a bit of risk for potentially higher rewards.
- **Growth:** Channel your inner mage, aiming to maximize capital appreciation. Growth stocks are for the adventurers willing to tackle higher risks for potentially grander rewards.
- **Trading/Speculation:** This is like choosing the swashbuckling pirate class. It's a high-risk strategy that seeks short-term profits through market acrobatics rather than focusing on long-term growth.

Your chosen quest and investment objectives determine your path in the financial game. You pick your character's abilities and set your objectives based on your financial goals and risk tolerance.

Balancing the Equation

Now, let's discuss creating the perfect mix in your financial game. Like choosing the right gear in a game, asset allocation is the first step. It's about dividing your investments among different asset classes, like stocks, bonds, or cash. Each class has its own risk and reward potential. Think of it as carefully selecting the skills for your game character.

Diversification is like having a well-balanced party of characters in your game squad. Investing in various assets within each class spreads the risk across different investments. Like in a game, if one character (or investment) faces a setback, others can step in to save the day.

Balancing risk and reward involves understanding your investment goals, risk tolerance, and available time. As you tailor your game strategy for your character's abilities, you craft your investment strategy to meet your financial goals.

Keeping an Eye on the Prize

In your financial journey, you must always keep an eye on the prize. This means regularly reviewing your investments, like checking your game stats. Experts recommend at least an annual review, especially during significant life changes or market events.

During these reviews, you should evaluate your portfolio's performance compared to benchmarks and assess individual assets. If assets are underperforming, it might be time to replace them with better-performing alternatives. It's like switching out your game equipment for better gear.

Mastering the Art of Rebalancing

Rebalancing is like adjusting your character's abilities based on the game's dynamics. It's about fine-tuning your asset allocation to maintain the desired balance of risk and return. Just as your character levels up, your portfolio must also level up.

Here are some strategies for rebalancing:

- **Periodic rebalancing:** You set a fixed time for annual reviews and adjustments. It's a steady approach to keep your portfolio on track.
- **Threshold rebalancing:** This strategy uses a percentage deviation from your target allocation as a trigger. For example, you rebalance when any asset deviates by five

percent or more. It helps keep the risk-reward balance intact.

- **Tactical rebalancing:** This is the dynamic approach, where you adjust based on market opportunities and your evolving financial situation. It's like upgrading your character's abilities during gameplay.

Remember, rebalancing may come with costs like taxes, fees, and commissions. Always weigh these costs against the potential benefits to find the most effective strategy for your unique financial journey.

Investing is a thrilling game, and mastering the art of risk and reward is critical to success. With asset allocation, diversification, and regular reviews, you can ensure your investments are on the right path. Just as in a game, the right strategy will lead you to victory in the world of finance.

So, get out there, fellow players, and make those well-informed moves. Level up your investment game, and may the rewards be ever in your favor!

RETIREMENT PLANNING

You might think retirement is light-years away, but trust me, it's never too early to start thinking about it. It sounds boring, but I promise it's important (Kagan, 2019).

What's Retirement Planning?

Okay, so retirement planning is all about getting ready for life after work. It's not just about money but also about deciding where you want to live, what you want to do, and when you want to stop working. It's like preparing for a super fun future!

Why Start Early?

The sooner you start, the better. Seriously, time is your superpower. The earlier you begin, the easier to save for your post-retirement dream life. Plus, you have more time for your money to grow and compound, so your savings can make more money for you!

How Much Do You Need?

People used to say you need a million bucks to retire comfortably. But everyone's situation is different. Consider how much you need based on your lifestyle, expenses, and goals. Remember to include housing, healthcare, and having fun! The key here is to personalize your plan.

Steps to Retirement Planning

1. **Make a Plan:** Start by deciding when you want to retire and what lifestyle you want. Think about what you'd like to do when you're not working, like traveling, hobbies, or just chilling. This will help you set a goal.
2. **Save Regularly:** Set aside money each month. Make it automatic to resist temptation. It's like setting aside some of your allowance or part-time job earnings. You'll thank yourself later for this discipline.
3. **Choose the Right Accounts:** Consider 401(k)s or IRAs. They come with tax benefits and free money from your employer. These accounts are like secret treasure chests that grow your money without as much tax, and your boss might even throw in extra cash as a bonus!
4. **Monitor Your Investments:** Keep an eye on how your money grows and make changes if needed. As you grow

older, your investment strategy may need to change. Sometimes, you should take less risk as you get closer to retirement.

Stages of Retirement Planning

- **Young Adulthood (21-35):** You have time on your side. Even small contributions can grow big over time. Compounding is your buddy. When you start early, your money has more time to grow, and that's like magic! Even a small amount of money invested now can turn into a big pot of gold later.
- **Early Midlife (36-50):** Life gets busy with mortgages and bills, but keep saving. Take advantage of employer plans and max out contributions. You're likely earning more at this stage, which means you can save more. So, take full advantage of employer plans and try to put away as much as possible.
- **Later Midlife (50-65):** Your investment accounts should become more conservative as you age. While time is running out, you can catch up with extra contributions. This is the time to ensure your investments are safe so you don't risk losing your savings right before retiring.

Other Aspects to Think About

- **Your Home:** Decide if you should sell or downsize when you retire. Your home can be a significant asset, but it also comes with costs. You might want to consider whether it's worth keeping a big house once your kids move out.
- **Estate Planning:** Make a will and consider strategies to minimize estate taxes. Estate planning ensures your assets go where you want them to after you're gone, and it can

also help your loved ones avoid paying a lot of taxes on what you leave behind.

- **Tax Efficiency:** Think about Roth accounts and consider a Roth conversion. Taxes can take a big bite out of your retirement savings, but there are strategies to minimize them. A Roth account can be a smart way to do this.
- **Insurance:** Explore Medicare, life insurance, and long-term care insurance. Health and financial protection are essential. These insurances can help you when you're older and might need more medical care or financial support.

Why Is Retirement Planning Important?

Retirement planning ensures you can enjoy life without working all the time. It's about maintaining your lifestyle, so you have the freedom to do what you love and secure your future. Imagine being able to travel, pursue your hobbies, and enjoy your time without financial worries.

So, even though retirement seems light-years away, planning for it now is the key to living your dream life later. Start early, make intelligent choices, and you'll be well on your way to a secure and fun retirement. Your future self will thank you!

ACTIVITY: RISK TOLERANCE QUESTIONNAIRE

1. Your best friend says his uncle will allow you to invest in a gold property. He says the investment will double before the end of the year. What do you do?

A. Weigh the risks and decide not to invest.
B. Invest $1,000, an amount you can afford to write off.

C. Get information about the company. If there's potential, invest $5,000.
D. Drain your savings to buy as many shares as possible.

2. You're getting a year-end bonus. You can take $700 cash or $800 in company stock, which you cannot sell for at least a year. In that time, the stock price could go up or down. What do you do?

A. Take the money while you can.
B. Take the stock because you believe in your company's potential.

3. A friend invites you to join a football pool with a $25 buy-in. You could win over $500. What do you do?

A. Say no thanks.
B. Ask another friend to split the cost since a $12.50 loss is better than a $25 loss.
C. Make some educated guesses and place your bet.

4. Your parents give you $10,000, asking that you invest it wisely. What do you do?

A. Buy the high-priced item you've had your eye on.
B. Put the cash in a safe-term deposit, earning two percent interest yearly.
C. Invest it all in a start-up company with huge potential rewards (and risks).
D. Get a financial adviser to help you diversify your investments.

5. A stock you bought a year ago has suddenly increased in value by 42%. What do you do?

A. Consider selling enough to cover your original investment.
B. Borrow money to buy more stock.
C. Sell and move your cash to a low-risk investment.

6. You receive an unexpected gift of $1,000. What do you do with it?

A. Save it in a low-risk savings account.
B. Invest it in a diversified portfolio of stocks and bonds.
C. Spend it on something you've been wanting.

7. You and your friends decide to start a small business together. The business idea is exciting, but it comes with significant financial risks. What's your initial reaction?

A. Express concerns about the financial risks and suggest a detailed business plan.
B. Show interest but seek advice from experienced entrepreneurs before committing.
C. Dive right in, excited about the potential rewards.

8. You're considering investing in a new cryptocurrency that has been making headlines for its rapid price increases. What's your approach?

A. Avoid it because you need more clarification about the risks and lack of information.
B. Invest a small amount after researching and understanding the risks.

C. Invest a significant portion of your savings to capitalize on the hype.

9. You have a part-time job, and your paycheck grew due to a raise. What do you do with the extra money?

A. Save it in a long-term savings account.
B. Invest it in a retirement account or college fund.
C. Spend it on entertainment and non-essential items.

10. You've been offered an opportunity to invest in a business venture with your classmates. The venture involves creating a new mobile app. What's your initial reaction?

A. Ask for a detailed business plan and consider the potential risks.
B. Express interest but request more information and potential return on investment.
C. Invest without hesitation because you believe in the idea.

11. Your older sibling advises you to start investing in the stock market, even though you're just a teenager. What's your response?

A. Show interest but prefer to start with safe and low-risk investments.
B. Invest in some of your savings and learn more about stock market basics.
C. Invest a significant amount because you're excited about the potential gains.

12. You win $500 in a local contest. What do you do with the prize money?

A. Save it for future expenses or emergencies.
B. Invest it in stocks or a college fund.
C. Spend it on a vacation or shopping spree.

Key to Determining Risk Tolerance:

- If you mainly chose **A responses**, you have a low-risk tolerance. You prefer safety and security in your financial decisions.
- You have a Moderate Risk Tolerance if you choose a mix of **A and B responses**. You are willing to take some financial risks but also value security.
- If you mainly chose **C responses**, you have a Moderate to High-Risk Tolerance. You are comfortable taking risks in your financial choices.
- If you mainly chose **D responses**, you have a High-Risk Tolerance. You are comfortable taking financial risks and may be a more aggressive investor.

This questionnaire and key can help you understand your natural tendencies regarding financial risk-taking (*Test Your Risk Tolerance - BCSC Investright*, 2016). You need to know your risk tolerance to make informed and responsible financial decisions (Grable & Lytton, 2020).

In this chapter, you have learned the basics about investments and the various types of investing you can explore to build your wealth. You've read about the risks and the rewards and even learned the importance of thinking and planning for retirement.

You would have learned a lot about yourself by completing the questionnaire, enough to get going with investing. This is the focus of the next chapter. Let's put what you have learned to work.

8

STARTING YOUR INVESTMENT JOURNEY

DOMINIC: THE TEENAGE SCOOTER MILLIONAIRE

A British teen, Dominic, became a millionaire by 13, thanks to a simple typo. He stumbled upon Viza, an American scooter company while searching for a "credit card visa." Eager to buy a scooter, he proposed distributing Viza scooters in the UK. They agreed, with a condition: sell five scooters, get the sixth free.

Determined, Dominic hustled to buy five scooters by selling gadgets in Japan. Soon, he was selling thousands of scooters weekly. His success caught the attention of Queen Elizabeth II, who appointed him a pioneer in British entrepreneurship. Today, Dominic serves on the Overseas Development Institute (ODI) board, inspiring others to seize opportunities and dream big (How to Become a Teenage Millionaire: 15 Success Stories, 2018).

INVESTMENT OPTIONS FOR TEENS AND YOUNG ADULTS

With all the information from the previous chapter buzzing in your head, I am sure you are more ready than ever to start your investment journey as soon as possible. In this chapter, we will explore Custodial accounts, Exchange-Traded Funds, and how Robo-Advisors have become a total game-changer in the world of investments.

Custodial Accounts

You might have heard about custodial accounts, but what's the deal? Well, let's break it down without all the boring grown-up jargon.

What's a Custodial Account?

It's like a savings account but with a twist (Segal, n.d.). An adult sets up a custodial account for someone under 18 (or 21, depending on where you live). That adult is the "custodian" and is in charge until you're old enough to take the wheel.

How Does It Work?

Once this account is up and running, it's like any other bank account or investment. The custodian, usually a responsible grown-up, decides how to invest the money. They can keep adding cash to the pot, too.

Types of Custodial Accounts

There are two types: UTMA and UGMA. What's the diff?

- Uniform Transfers to Minors Act (UTMA) accounts: Hold various assets, including real estate and art.
- Uniform Gift to Minors Act (UGMA) accounts: Limited to financial assets like cash, securities, annuities, and insurance policies.

The Perks

Here's the fun part: These accounts are super flexible, with no income limits, no annoying rules about when you can take money out, and no penalties. You can even use the cash for stuff like housing and clothes. No boring college-only spending rules!

Tax Talk

When it comes to taxes, it's a win-win for you. The IRS sees you as the boss of this account, so you get taxed at your lower kiddo rate. That means more cash in your pocket. Plus, for 2023, you can put up to $17,000 there without worrying about gift taxes.

Anything to Watch Out For?

Well, there's always a catch, right? Having this account might affect how much college aid you can get, and you can't change the beneficiary once it's set up. But hey, that's the trade-off for the perks.

The Big Moment

When you hit the big 1-8 (or 2-1), the account is all yours, and you can do whatever you want with it. So, if you're ready to take control of your moolah, custodial accounts are a sweet way to start your money adventure.

Always talk to a financial whiz-kid or a grown-up before diving into the money world. Stay smart, and happy savings!

EXCHANGE-TRADED FUNDS (ETFS)

Investing is a maze of complex choices, especially for teens just starting. The good news is there's a simple and smart way to dip your toes into investments: Exchange-Traded Funds (ETFs). Think of them as your passport to the world of financial growth and security (*Teen Investors Exchange-Traded Funds*, n.d.).

What Are ETFs?

Exchange-traded funds, or ETFs for short, are like a basket of different goodies. They bundle together a diverse group of stocks, bonds, or other assets and trade on the stock market like individual stocks. ETFs have been around for a few decades, making them a relatively new but handy way to invest.

Why ETFs for Teens?

You might be wondering, "Why choose ETFs?" Well, ETFs are perfect for teens who don't have endless hours to research individual stocks or tons of money to spare. Here's why:

- **Affordable for Everyone:** ETFs can be bought for as little as $5. Yep, you read that right! Fractional share investing allows you to own a piece of an ETF without breaking the bank.
- **Diversification Magic:** ETFs are like financial wizards. They spread your money across many companies, lowering the risk of one company's troubles sinking your investment ship. It's like investing without putting all your eggs in one basket.

Flavors of ETFs

ETFs come in various flavors, much like an ice cream shop. Some follow the stock market, some deal with bonds, and there are even ETFs for things like cryptocurrencies, gold, real estate, and more. But for teens, it's best to stick to index-based ETFs. These mimic the performance of major market indexes and are less risky.

Top 3 Index-Based ETFs for Teens

- **Vanguard 500 Index Fund (Symbol: VOO):** This ETF follows the Standard and Poor's 500 Index, which tracks the top 500 US companies. It's like owning a slice of the entire American business pie.
- **SPDR Dow Jones Industrial Average ETF Trust (Symbol: DIA):** This ETF mirrors the Dow Jones Industrial Average, which includes 30 large US companies. It's like having a piece of the oldest stock club in town.
- **Invesco QQQ Trust (Symbol: QQQ):** This ETF represents the NASDAQ index, which is all about high-tech stocks. It's like investing in the future of technology.

Where to Get Info

To make informed investment decisions, you need information. Websites like Finance.yahoo.com are your best friends. Search for an ETF using its symbol (like VOO, DIA, or QQQ), and you'll find details about its price, performance, and top holdings.

The Expense Ratio

Investing isn't free, but you want to avoid paying a fortune to invest, right? That's where the expense ratio comes in. It covers the cost of managing the ETF. For broad index-based ETFs, like the ones we recommend, the expense ratios are low, around 0.03% to 0.20%. That's a tiny price to pay for a smart investment.

The Power of Long-Term Gains

It's important to understand that ETFs can offer solid returns over time. While they might dip occasionally, their long-term track record tends to be positive. Think of it as planting a tree that will provide you with financial shade in the future.

So, if you're looking for a way to invest that's straightforward, affordable, and has a strong potential for growth, give ETFs a try.

FRACTIONAL SHARE INVESTING

Investing might sound like something only grown-ups with a ton of cash can do, but guess what? You can start investing with just a few bucks, and it's all thanks to something called fractional shares (Davis, n.d.).

So, What Exactly Are Fractional Shares?

Fractional shares are like the appetizers of the stock market world. Instead of buying a whole pizza, you can get just a slice. It's the same with stocks. You don't have to buy a whole share; you can own a piece. Let's break it down with a simple example: Imagine you have $100, and one share of a fancy tech company costs $75. If you couldn't buy fractional shares, you'd be stuck with nothing or the whole share. With fractional shares, you can buy a fraction of a share for as little as $5.00. So, let's say Tesla is $300 a share; you could put $30 in and get 0.10 of a share or 10% of a share. You will earn 10% of any increase and lose 10% of any decrease, and if it pays a dividend of, say, $1.00 for the full share, you will earn 10 cents. Cool, right?

Why Should Teens Care About Fractional Shares?

- **Diversification Magic:** If you want to build a collection of different stocks, but each one is super expensive, fractional shares are your ticket. You can spread your money across various companies, even if you don't have a mountain of cash. It's like building a delicious sampler platter instead of eating just one dish.
- **Small Investments, Big Gains:** Imagine a stock you love that costs a fortune, like a new gaming console. Fractional shares let you buy a part of it, making investing possible without emptying your wallet. Whether it's $5, $50, or $500, you can start small and watch your investment grow over time.
- **Stay in the Game:** Fractional shares are like your trusty sidekick when you invest a fixed monthly amount. If the stock you want costs more than your monthly budget, you'd usually end up with cash just sitting around. But

fractional shares let you use every penny you've got for investing. No more idle cash!

But Is There a Catch?

Here's the deal: Transferring fractional shares can be tricky if you decide to switch to a different platform or broker. You might have to sell them first, which could mean dealing with taxes or fees. Also, remember that investing is a long-term game. Don't let fractional shares tempt you into constantly buying and selling; that usually doesn't work out.

So, investing isn't just for the rich and famous. You can start small and watch your money grow over time, thanks to fractional shares. It's like having a little piece of the financial pie, and you enjoy every bite! Happy investing!

Let's let you in on a little secret. I look at my stocks daily and plan ahead by reading about what's going on with the company. When stocks take a nosedive, that's the best time to buy if it's a solid company because when it goes back up, voila, cha-ching!

INDEX-BASED ETFS

A great way to cut your teeth in the investing game is through Index funds (Modu, 2023). ETFs and index funds diverge in their trading mechanisms. Like stocks, ETFs permit trading throughout the day, offering flexibility in buying and selling. In contrast, index funds are subject to transactions at a fixed price established at the close of the trading day, limiting the window for buying and selling activities.

What Are Index Funds Anyway?

Index funds are like a super cool basket of different stocks. Imagine you want a bit of every candy at the candy store; that's what index funds do with stocks. These funds aim to match the performance of a market index, like the S&P 500, which includes the 500 largest companies in the United States. They're like the 'greatest hits' of the stock market.

Why Should Teens Consider Index Funds?

- **Diversification for the Win:** Diversification is like not putting all your eggs in one basket. With index funds, your money is spread across many different stocks. If one stock has a bad day, it won't sink your entire investment ship.
- **Protection Against Rollercoaster Rides:** Suppose you bought a famous tech company's stock, like Amazon, and it took a nosedive. Ouch! But your loss would've been less if you'd invested in an index fund like the Vanguard 500 Index Fund, which follows the S&P 500. Index funds are like the safety harness on a financial rollercoaster.
- **Simple and Cost-Effective:** Index funds are low-maintenance. You don't need to hire a pro to manage them because they aim to match the market, not beat it. Plus, they come with lower fees compared to some fancy-schmancy investment options.

Mutual Funds Versus Exchange-Traded Funds

Now, let's talk about two close cousins of index funds: mutual funds and exchange-traded funds (ETFs). Both of them include a bunch of stocks, just like index funds. But there's a big difference for teens: mutual funds often need a hefty upfront investment, sometimes as much as $3,000.

That's a lot of allowance to part with!

On the other hand, ETFs are your go-to choice. They work like magic for teen investors because they have a lower entry cost. As discussed earlier, you can invest as little as $5 in an ETF using an online broker that allows fractional shares. So, you see, you don't have to wait until you become a high-roller to have an investment portfolio!

ROBO-ADVISORS

Robo-advisors have been making waves in the world of finance for a few years now. Thanks to companies like Wealthfront and Betterment, these digital investing gurus are changing the game (Abella, 2023). But what's all the buzz about, and why are they incredibly cool for young investors?

What's a Robo-Advisor, Anyway?

Think of a Robo-Advisor as your digital money mentor. These savvy systems make investing super easy, and they're perfect for beginners or young investors. They're like your personal GPS for the stock market, helping you navigate the investing journey.

Why Young Investors Love Robo-Advisors

Young investors, that's us, often find Robo-Advisors especially appealing. Here's why:

1. **Easy Peasy:** Robo-advisors are as easy as playing your favorite video game. Some apps and websites have user-

friendly interfaces that make setting up your investments a breeze. Take Betterment, for example, where you can set your retirement goals within minutes or even explore crypto portfolios. It's like swiping right for investing success!

2. **Say Goodbye to In-Person Appointments:** In this digital age, we like doing things online, right? Robo-Advisors get it. No need to make an appointment with a human, financial advisor; you can do everything online. Just fill out some forms, and the Robo-Advisor does the rest. Your money, your way.
3. **Invest with Your Pocket Money:** Got a little extra cash from your allowance? With Robo-Advisors, you can start investing with as little as $1. That's right; even if you find some spare change in your piggy bank, you can put it to work. Plus, some Robo-Advisors have super low minimum contributions.
4. **Making Every Cent Work:** The cool thing about attaching a Robo-Advisor to your banking account is that it will round up what you spend and, once it gets to $5, invest in the market. I like this because it's money you can take advantage of.
5. **Less Cost, More Savings:** Robo-advisors are the budget-friendly superheroes of investing. They usually have low fees, and some even offer free trades. Traditional human advisors can charge hefty fees, often one percent or more of your investments. With Robo-Advisors, you get advice without breaking the bank.
6. **Trust in Technology:** We've grown up in the digital age, and for many of us, robots are more trustworthy than humans. Some people think machines are less likely to mess things up. Plus, there have been stories of financial advisors getting into trouble. Robots seem more reliable.

7. **Smart Money Moves:** The best Robo-Advisors have awesome features like tax-loss harvesting and automatic portfolio rebalancing. These services were once reserved for the rich folks who worked with elite financial advisors. Now, Robo-Advisors lets average investors like us access these cool strategies.

Special Lingo to Know

Alright, young investors, here's some unique lingo you should be familiar with when using Robo-Advisors:

1. **Portfolio:** Imagine this as your array of investments. It encompasses stocks, bonds, and other assets you decide to invest in.
2. **Diversification:** Picture this as the strategy of not putting all your resources into a single avenue. Diversification involves spreading your investments across a range of asset types to mitigate risk.
3. **Asset Allocation:** This is like a recipe for your investments. It's the mix of different assets in your portfolio. For example, you might have 60% stocks and 40% bonds in your asset allocation.
4. **Risk Tolerance:** This measures your comfort with taking risks. A higher risk tolerance means you're okay with potentially higher ups and downs in your investments.
5. **Rebalancing:** Imagine you have a pizza with different toppings. Rebalancing is like ensuring each topping is in the right proportion so your pizza tastes great. In investing, it's adjusting your portfolio back to your target asset allocation.

6. **ETFs:** These are like bundles of stocks or bonds. When you invest in an ETF, you're getting a piece of many different assets at once.
7. **Cryptocurrency:** It's digital money, like Bitcoin. Some Robo-Advisors let you include cryptocurrencies in your portfolio.

What to Keep In Mind

Robo-advisors are like having a personal financial assistant. They help, but they're not a magical money-making machine. Here are some things to remember:

- **New Kids on the Block:** Robo-advisors are still relatively new compared to traditional investing. Deep market recessions haven't tested them, and their ability to tackle rising prices is still a question mark.
- **Learning the Lingo:** Investing can feel like learning a new language. Robo-advisors are beginner-friendly, but it's good to understand some of the jargon and concepts used in the industry.
- **Returns Vary:** The returns you get depend on the Robo-Advisor you choose and the investment portfolio you go for. According to The Robo Report, returns ranged from around 2.84% to 5.12% in 2022 for a typical portfolio. So, it's not always rainbows and unicorns, but they're built to handle economic rollercoasters.
- **The Hybrid Option:** Some brokerages offer a mix of Robo-Advisors and human advisors. It's like getting the best of both worlds. You can chat with a human when you need advice but still enjoy the low cost and convenience of Robo-Advisors.

So, Why Are Young People Flocking to Robo-Advisors?

Robo-Advisors are a hit with the younger crowd for a bunch of reasons. We tend to trust technology more, and we love doing things online. Robo-advisors make investing accessible and fun, even if you're starting with a small amount of money.

Who Should Use Robo-Advisors?

If you're new to investing, want a simple and affordable way to start, and are okay not talking to humans, Robo-Advisors are your besties. But if you have complex financial needs or want a personal touch, traditional advisors might be more your style.

Robo-advisors are like the sidekicks of the investing world. They're low-cost, easy to use, and ideally suited for tech-savvy young investors. Plus, they're open 24/7; no appointment is needed! If you're curious about investing, these digital money mentors are here to guide you.

ACTIVITY: WHAT IS YOUR INVESTMENT STYLE?

Answer these 10 questions to uncover your investing style and get a sense of your financial personality.

1. How long would you expect to invest before you need access to funds?

A – Very short term (the next six months)
B – Short term (the next 12–18 months)
C – Short to medium term (the next 18 months to three years)
D – Medium term (the next three to five years)

E – Medium to long term (the next five to ten years)
F – Long term (more than ten years)

2. What type of investments have your previous (or current) investments been?

A – I only have investment experience in basic banking products and term deposits (i.e., never invested in bonds, shares, or property).
B – I have had minimal exposure to basic banking products, bonds, and property.
C – I have had some investment experience and some exposure to property and equities.
D – I have had some experience in all major asset classes, including Australian shares, as well as some minimal experience with international shares.
E – I have had a lot of experience in all asset classes, with a particular focus on Australian and international shares.
F – I have had a great deal of experience in all asset classes, including the overseas share markets and 'exotic' investment products, such as artwork or luxury cars.

3. Which of the following best describes your investment objectives?

A – To generate an income without reinvesting dividends.
B – To generate an income and a small amount of growth.
C – To generate an equal amount of income and growth.
D – To generate a small amount of income and have substantial growth.
E – To generate growth with little to no income.
F – To achieve growth without receiving income, you consistently reinvest your dividends to maximize the bene-

fits of compound interest, ensuring the highest potential income upon retirement.
To generate growth with no income. (This means you're constantly reinvesting your dividends to take full advantage of compound interest, leaving you with the highest possible income at retirement.)

4. Suppose your investment strategy was for the long term (minimum seven to ten years). How would you react if, in six months, your portfolio decreased in value by 20%?

A – I would not accept any declines in the value of my investment portfolio.
B – I would transfer my investments to more stable investment markets.
C – I would be somewhat concerned but can accept very short-term market volatility.
D – I would adopt a 'wait and see' approach to see if the investments improve before deciding.
E – I know the risks and volatility levels are higher, so I would leave the original long-term strategy in place to let it run its course.
F – As I expect long-term growth, I would intend to invest more money to take advantage of the lower average investment prices.

5. How would you describe your risk tolerance when it comes to investments?

A – I'm very risk-averse and prefer minimal to no risk, even if it means lower potential returns.
B – I'm somewhat risk-averse, prioritizing stability and moderate returns.

C – I have a balanced approach to risk; I'm willing to accept some risk for the opportunity of higher returns.
D – I have a higher risk tolerance and aim for substantial returns, even if it involves more significant risk.
E – I'm extremely risk-tolerant and prioritize the potential for maximum returns, even if it means accepting substantial risk.

6. How would you react to a sudden, significant drop in the stock market?

A – I would immediately sell my investments to limit my losses.
B – I would feel concerned but wait to see if the market recovers.
C – I might consider adjusting my portfolio, but I would largely stay the course.
D – I see market drops as potential buying opportunities and would consider investing more.
E – I wouldn't be too bothered as I have a long-term perspective, and market fluctuations are normal.

7. Regarding investment fees, which statement resonates with you the most?

A – I'm willing to pay higher fees for professional advice and management.
B – I prefer to keep my fees low and use low-cost investment options.
C – I'm open to a balance; fees are necessary, but so is professional guidance.
D – I prioritize keeping fees low and tend to favor self-directed investing.

E – Fees don't concern me much; I focus on potential returns.

8. How closely do you monitor your investments?

A – I check my investments daily, sometimes multiple times a day.
B – I review my investments weekly or when significant news arises.
C – I check my investments monthly to ensure they align with my goals.
D – I take a quarterly approach, reviewing my portfolio every few months.
E – I prefer a hands-off approach, checking my investments annually or less often.

9. Regarding asset allocation, what is the most important factor for your investment strategy?

A – Capital preservation and minimizing risk.
B – Steady income and lower volatility.
C – A balanced approach with a mix of growth and stability.
D – Capital growth and achieving market-beating returns.
E – Maximizing growth potential, even if it means accepting higher volatility.

10. Which best describes your perspective on investment research?

A – I rely on expert advice and in-depth research.
B – I do some research but appreciate guidance.
C – I perform moderate research and prefer a mix of information sources.

D – I'm a DIY investor and conduct extensive research independently.
E – I trust my instincts and prefer limited research.

Results: Add up the number of times you chose each letter:

A. _____
B. _____
C. _____
D. _____
E. _____
F. _____

Investor Type:

A – You're a defensive investor.
B – You're a conservative investor.
C – You're a moderate conservative investor.
D – You're a moderate grower.
E – You're a growth investor.
F – You're a high-growth investor.

Knowing how far you are willing to go and what you can comfortably risk is undoubtedly a giant step toward financial freedom. In this chapter, you learned about the most suitable types of investment opportunities you should look into and the pros and cons of each. After taking the above quiz, you should have a pretty good idea of your investment personality or character.

All that is left to do now is earn some moolah! The next chapter deals with your earning power and how to ensure you are paid at competitive rates.

PART III

NAVIGATING INCOME POTENTIAL

9

UNLEASHING YOUR ENTREPRENEURIAL SPIRIT

At just 15 years old, Cory Nieves is well on his way to a net worth of over $1 million (£769k). His story is a beacon of hope for serious-minded teens seeking wealth (*The Teen Millionaires Making Their Own Fortune*, 2020).

Cory's journey began at six with a simple goal: buy his mom a car so they wouldn't have to rely on the bus. His strategy? A bake sale. What made it extraordinary? Cory's determination.

He decided to sell coffee and cookies, but not just any cookies, his cookies. His recipe was a hit, and after perfecting it, Cory and his mom launched "Mr. Cory's Cookies" in a commercial kitchen. The power of social media and community support propelled their brand to new heights. Cory's story teaches us that age is no barrier to success. For teens seeking wealth, Cory's journey shows that passion, determination, and creativity can turn dreams into reality.

Cory Nieves, at 15, proves that the recipe for success is within reach, waiting for you to mix your passion with perseverance to create something extraordinary.

HOW TO START YOUR BUSINESS

For all you aspiring business tycoons reading this, school is the perfect time to start your entrepreneurial journey, and here's the inside scoop on some business ideas and top tips for creating and growing your very own venture (*Empowering Teen Entrepreneurs: A Comprehensive Guide - Crimson Education ZA*, 2023). Let's make those dreams of wealth and success a reality!

Unleash Your Passion and Skills

First things first, discover what fuels your passions. What gets your heart racing? What are you naturally good at? Your business venture should be an extension of your interests and talents. Combining your passions with your strengths makes the journey more fun and your chances of success even greater.

Craft a Unique Selling Proposition

Here's the deal: You need a unique selling proposition (USP) to stand out. What sets your product or service apart from the competition? It's one thing that makes people say, "I need this!" To create a compelling USP, understand your target audience's needs and analyze your competitors' strengths and weaknesses. Then, select key differentiators that genuinely set you apart from the crowd.

Network Locally

Connecting with local businesses and organizations is like gold for your business. Attend local events, join clubs or associations, and be active on social media. Building relationships with fellow entrepreneurs can offer valuable insights, support, and opportunities that can supercharge your business growth.

Dazzle With Customer Service

Exceptional customer service is the secret sauce to success. Be prompt, friendly, and attentive to your customers' needs. Show them you genuinely care. Happy customers keep coming back and bring in new business through word-of-mouth. This is like compounding but with people instead of money!

Seek Wisdom From Mentors

Don't shy away from seeking mentorship. A mentor is like a Jedi master guiding a young Padawan (you). They've been there and done that, and they can help you navigate the business galaxy. Find a mentor who inspires you, shares your goals, and can provide insights based on their experiences.

Being an entrepreneur means facing challenges, and they're part of the game. Stay persistent in the face of obstacles and be adaptable. Learn from your mistakes; everyone makes them.

Remember, flexibility is your secret weapon in the ever-changing world of business.

Business Ideas for High School Trailblazers

Now, onto some business ideas that are a perfect fit for high school entrepreneurs:

1. **Tutoring Service:** Use your academic strengths to help your peers. Tutoring earns you cash and builds confidence

and vital skills like communication and leadership. Consider turning your knowledge into a course you can sell online.

2. **Custom Merchandise:** Unleash your creativity by designing custom apparel for school clubs, teams, or events. This venture hones your design skills, project coordination, and customer communication.
3. **Event Planning:** Organize school events like dances or fundraisers. This builds your organizational and teamwork skills while creating memorable experiences for your school.
4. **Social Media Consulting:** Leverage your digital savviness to help clubs, local businesses, or individuals manage social media. You'll gain experience in content creation, branding, and audience engagement.
5. **Art and Design:** Turn your artistic talents into a profitable venture. Offer services like custom illustrations, graphic design, or logo creation. This helps you develop time management, project coordination, and client communication skills.
6. **Charitable Initiative:** Make a positive impact on your community by creating a social enterprise that supports local causes. This demonstrates your empathy, leadership, and problem-solving skills while making the world a better place.

Incorporate these ideas into your school journey, and you'll make some money and gain valuable skills and experiences that will set you on the path to wealth and success. Balancing academics with business is challenging, but it's a rewarding adventure that will shape you into the next generation of business leaders. So, go out there and chase your dreams while still in school; your future self will thank you for it!

THE BENEFITS OF STARTING YOUR OWN BUSINESS

School isn't just about textbooks and tests; it's the perfect time to unleash your inner entrepreneur. Starting your own business might seem daunting, but let us walk you through 10 fantastic reasons you should consider taking the plunge (Shank, 2015).

1. Valuable Life Lessons

Starting a business isn't just about making money; it serves as a comprehensive introduction to fundamental life skills. Throughout this experience, you will acquire essential attributes such as responsibility, perseverance, diligence, honesty, integrity, effective time management, leadership capabilities, and improved communication skills. Success isn't always easy or glamorous, but it's a brilliant teacher.

2. Acquire Time Management Skills

Entrepreneurs frequently dedicate extended hours to their work due to their enthusiasm. This necessity leads them to become adept at time management. Identifying your individual rhythm and cultivating self-discipline are essential skills that prove to be beneficial across various aspects of life.

3. Set Your Schedule and Pursue Passion

Imagine a world where you create your own schedule while doing what you love. Whether crafting, designing, or blogging, entrepreneurship lets you turn your passions into profits. It won't always feel like work, and that's the beauty of it.

4. Enhance Communication and Presentation

In business, clear communication and professionalism are the keys to success. How you present yourself, both online and offline, is vital. It's not just about what you say but how you say it.

Dress appropriately, maintain a respectful online presence, and remember that first impressions matter.

5. Build Connections

Networking isn't just a buzzword; it's essential for future opportunities. As a young entrepreneur, you can connect with bloggers, local business owners, and potential employers. These connections can be your stepping stones to future success.

6. Earn Your Own Money

Earning your own money brings a sense of pride and independence. It's your chance to be financially responsible and self-reliant. Plus, it's excellent preparation for the future when college or car expenses loom.

7. Learn Financial Management

The business world has its own lingo: profit, loss, cost of goods sold, and gross/net profit. Understanding these terms equips you with essential financial knowledge that isn't just handy for your business and life.

8. Portfolio and Distinction

Launching your own business sets you apart and enhances your portfolio. It shows initiative and a go-getter attitude that employers and colleges love. This is your chance to shine in a sea of high school accomplishments.

9. Teen Entrepreneurs Can Change the World

This generation is the future, and teens are known for their fearlessness. Take calculated risks, and you'll be amazed at the impact you can have. Don't be afraid to start when you're young; history is full of successful young entrepreneurs who went on to shape the world.

10. It's Fun

Despite the challenges, entrepreneurship can be incredibly fun and fulfilling. While others are shopping every weekend, you're building your future. Every step you take in your business journey is a step towards a more exciting and fulfilling life.

In a world where 40% of teens want to start their own business but only 3% actually do, why not be among those who dare to dream? Starting your business as a teen might seem like a small step, but it could lead to something huge. Take that leap of faith and discover the endless possibilities out there.

So, are you ready to embark on your entrepreneurial journey and learn lessons that textbooks can't teach? Go on, make your dreams a reality!

ACTIVITY: CREATE A BUSINESS PLAN

Feel free to adapt this template to get your brilliant new business idea up and running. You can also check out some great online resources for business plans. Find the one that suits your ideas best.

Business Plan Template

Business Name: ______________________________

Teen Entrepreneur: ___________________________

Date: ____________________________________

Executive Summary

Business Concept

Briefly describe your business idea. What products or services will you offer? Explain the inspiration behind your business.

Mission Statement

What is the core purpose of your business? What values and principles will guide your business?

Vision Statement

Where do you see your business in the future? What are your long-term goals?

Business Description

Business Background

Explain how your business idea came about.

Discuss any experience or skills you have related to this business.

Market Research

Describe your target market (age, interests, location, etc.). Analyze your competitors and their strengths and weaknesses.

Explain how your business will meet the needs of your target market better than your competitors.

Feel free to see what AI can come up with, too.

Products or Services

Product/Service Description

Detail the products or services you'll provide.

Highlight any unique features or benefits of your products/services.

Pricing Strategy

Explain your pricing strategy. How will you determine your prices? Are there any special offers or discounts you plan to offer?

Marketing and Sales Marketing Strategy

Explain how you plan to market your business to attract customers. Include online and offline marketing strategies.

Sales Strategy

Describe how you will make sales.

If applicable, discuss any partners or sales channels.

Operations and Management

Business Location

Describe where your business will operate. Will it be online, from home, or at a physical location?

Staffing

If you plan to hire employees or seek help from family and friends, outline your staffing needs.

Financial Projections

Startup Costs

List the initial expenses needed to get your business up and running. Include costs for equipment, supplies, licenses, and marketing.

Sales Forecasts

Estimate your expected sales over the next year.

Break this down into months.

Profit and Loss Statement

Create a basic income statement, including revenues, costs, and expenses. Cash Flow Projection

Detail your expected cash flow for the first year.

Funding Requirements

Funding Needs

Explain if you need external financing (loans, investments) and how much. Use of Funds

Describe how you plan to use the funds if acquired. (e.g., marketing, equipment purchase) Appendices

Supporting Documents

Attach any additional documents that support your business plan. These may include resumes, market research data, or legal documents.

Remember, a business plan is a dynamic document that can change as your business evolves. It is a roadmap to guide your efforts and secure financing if needed. Starting a business without a plan is like driving across the country to a destination you've never been to without any GPS or guide. Good luck with your entrepreneurial journey!

With your business ideas flowing and the business plan coming together in a way that would make even Elon Musk proud, you will be all set to give him a run for his money.

Unfortunately, there is a vicious monster that you should be on the lookout for. It will chew you up and spit you out until all that's left are shards of the exuberant business go-getter you started off as. Okay, so maybe I am being somewhat dramatic here. Still, you should pay attention to the next chapter on debt and how to manage it. Most new startups go belly up due to relying more on borrowed funds than they see in returns by the end of the first year or even a few months in business.

PART IV

DEMYSTIFYING DEBIT AND CREDIT

10

THE PITFALLS OF TOO MUCH DEBT

Imagine being just nine years old and simply wanting lip balm. Most of us would've given up after our parents said no, but not Zandra Cunningham. She didn't just make her own lip balm; she created a thriving beauty empire, Zandra Beauty (Squad, 2021b).

Zandra's journey is a testament to the power of determination and creativity. As a teenager, she managed her business and made it a force for good. She became an advocate for girls' education, contributing 10% of her profits to support young women in pursuing STEAM education and entrepreneurship worldwide.

But that's not all. Zandra didn't back down when the world faced the challenges of a pandemic. She adapted, shifting from B2B to e-commerce sales and even re-tooling her manufacturing to create cruelty-free hand sanitizers.

Zandra's story teaches us that age is just a number when it comes to pursuing your dreams. It's a reminder that you can achieve incredible things with passion, hard work, and a desire to make a positive impact. So, if you're a teen with a dream, take inspiration from Zandra's story and remember that anything is possible when you put your mind to it. Start small, think big, and let your passion drive you to success.

UNDERSTANDING GOOD DEBT VERSUS BAD DEBT

Debt can be a daunting word, especially for teenagers who are beginning to explore personal finance. But it's crucial to understand that not all debts are created equal. Some debts can be a valuable tool that helps you achieve your goals, while others can become a financial nightmare. Let's dive deeper into good vs. bad debt to help you make informed financial choices (Pyles, n.d.).

Good Debt - Investing in Your Future

Good debt is an investment in yourself or your future. Here are some examples:

1. **Student Loans:** Education is a powerful asset; student loans can open doors to better job opportunities. Federal student loans often have lower interest rates, making them a manageable investment. When taking on student loans, keep your monthly payment below 10% of your projected income after graduation.
2. **Mortgages:** Buying a home is a significant financial decision. To determine how much house you can afford, your mortgage payment should be at most 36% of your income. If it exceeds that, consider options like downsizing or refinancing.
3. **Car Loans:** For many, having a car is essential for daily life. Ensure your total auto costs, including your car loan payment, stay within 20% of your take-home pay.

Bad Debt - Financial Pitfalls to Avoid

Bad debt can hinder your financial well-being and even lead to a crisis. Here are some examples of bad debts you will want to avoid at all costs:

High-Interest Credit Cards

Accumulating debt on high-interest credit cards, typically with rates over 20%, can be financially dangerous. To manage this type of debt, consider strategies like the debt snowball method or using balance transfer cards to lower your interest costs.

Personal Loans for Discretionary Expenses

Taking on debt for non-essential purchases, like vacations or luxury items, can become expensive. If you need help with such loans, look into refinancing options.

Refinancing is like hitting the reset button on a loan or mortgage. When you refinance, you're changing the loan rules to your advantage. It's similar to adjusting the settings in a video game. You can change your interest rate and payment schedule or switch from one type of loan to another. People refinance for various reasons. If interest rates drop, you can save money by getting a better deal, just like a discount in a game. If your financial situation improves, you might qualify for better loan terms, like leveling up in a game.

Sometimes, life's surprises require financial plan adjustments, and refinancing helps. If you're managing multiple loans, refinancing can consolidate them into one, making your financial life simpler to handle. Like in a game, you can change your approach for better results. But remember, it's always wise to consult a financial expert before hitting that refinancing "reset" button (Alexandra Twin, 2021).

Payday Loans

These short-term, high-interest loans can quickly trap you in a cycle of debt. Financial experts advise against payday loans. Instead, explore alternatives such as borrowing from a credit union or seeking help from family members.

In summary, good debt can serve as a stepping stone toward your dreams, while bad debt can become a heavy anchor that hinders your financial progress. Managing your debt responsibly and making well-informed financial decisions as you navigate your path to financial independence is essential. Remember that financial literacy is your best friend when making intelligent financial choices.

AVOIDING THE PITFALLS OF TOO MUCH DEBT

Try following these simple yet effective tips for managing your finances so that you side-step the snare of debt. It is a life sentence for many grown-ups, and it starts with learning proper money management skills in your teen years (*10 Strategies to Avoid Getting into Debt | Central Bank*, n.d.)

- **Cash is King:** Don't use your card if you can't afford it with cash. Don't fall into the trap of thinking your credit card is magic money. You can't afford it if you don't have the cash.
- **Build an Emergency Fund:** Start saving for unexpected situations. Aim for at least three to six months of expenses.

It's like having extra lives in a video game for when things get tough.

- **Pay Credit Card Balances ASAP:** Make it a habit to pay off your credit card balances as soon as possible. Don't let those interest charges creep up on you. Here's a pro tip: Find a credit card option with a cash-back option for each purchase and no annual fee. Then, use their money but pay it back in full each month from your earnings. In this way, you earn money to cover your regular monthly expenses! Over time, this could add up to a decent sum of moolah!
- **Distinguish Wants from Needs:** It's fun to treat yourself, but cutting back on non-essential spending is a smart move. Reserve those special treats for rare occasions.
- **Create a Budget:** Keep track of your expenses by setting up a monthly budget. This helps you see where your money goes and ensures you save for the future.
- **No Cash Advances:** Using your credit card for cash advances is a no-no. High-interest rates and fees can get you into a tricky financial maze.
- **Limit Your Credit Cards:** Don't juggle multiple credit cards. Stick to one or two to avoid confusion and overspending. It's like trying to complete one level at a time in a game.
- **Expense Tracker:** Maintain a record of your expenses in a spreadsheet. This way, you won't forget any bills and can avoid late fees.
- **Save Pay Increases:** Don't inflate your lifestyle when you get a pay raise. Save the extra money instead. You've already proven you can live on your previous income, so put the extra in savings for your future goals.
- **Coupon Magic:** Coupons aren't just for your parents. Use them to save on your must-have items. The money you save can be a safety net for unexpected expenses.

Remember, avoiding debt might be challenging, but it's a game you can win with these strategies. You'll have financial freedom and still some money to treat yourself occasionally.

ACTIVITY: QUIZ ON GOOD DEBT VERSUS BAD DEBT

Are you ready to try your hand at a quick and easy quiz on telling good debt from bad? Let's see how you do (Kunze, 2016).

1. How is debt defined?

a) Money someone owes you.
b) Money that is owed.
c) Money that will increase in value over time.
d) Money that will decrease in value over time.

2. Which of the following is an example of good debt?

a) Buying a car.
b) Buying a bike.
c) Buying a bus pass.
d) Taking out a student loan to pay for postsecondary school.

3. Is debt ever a good thing?

a) Yes, because some kinds of debt are associated with appreciating assets.
b) No, it is never good to owe money.

4. What is bad debt?

a) Bad debt is when the percentage you pay on the loan is high.
b) Bad debt is money you owe associated with depreciating assets.
c) Bad debt is owing any money.

5. Are student loans generally an example of good debt or bad debt?

a) Good debt
b) Bad debt

6. When might student loans be an example of bad debt?

a) When you must borrow money to pay for tuition and books.
b) When you borrow more money for college than you need.
c) When you borrow money from the government.

7. Why are student loans generally considered good debt?

a) You learn a lot in college.
b) Taking on student loans to obtain a higher education often results in landing a better career, increasing your earning potential.
c) You meet great people in college.
d) The cost of college is decreasing.

8. Is business debt an example of good or bad debt?

a) Good
b) Bad

9. Which of the following is an example of bad debt?

a) Buying a car with a loan.
b) Buying furniture.
c) Carrying money over from month to month on a credit card.
d) All of these are bad debts.

10. Why is paying off the entire credit card balance after 30 days important?

a) If you do not, you will have to pay interest on top of what you owe.
b) The credit card companies will suspend your account.
c) Your interest rate will increase.
d) Paying off your entire monthly credit card bill is unimportant.

11. Why is it recommended that credit card users pay their bills on time?

a) The amount you owe will double if your bill is not paid on time.
b) Actually, there is no due date for credit card bills.
c) If your bill is not paid on time, interest starts to accrue

12. True or false: Credit cards not paid off monthly are an example of bad debt.

a) True
b) False

13. How do credit card companies make a lot of their money?

a) They charge high fees for credit cards.
b) They sell products people want.
c) They count on the fact that many people will carry a balance on their card and thus make money from the interest.

14. What does it mean to "live like a student while in college so you don't have to later?"

a) Have a lot of fun in college.
b) Spend money how you see fit in college.
c) Study as hard as you can in college.
d) Live simply in college, do not overspend, and do well in college so that the benefits of a college degree pay off for you later in life.

15. Why might credit card companies target college students?

a) College students tend to need more experience managing their money and may make mistakes.
b) College students need some way to pay for necessities.
c) They tend to make money off college students' credit cards.
d) All answers are correct.

Answer Sheet:

1. b) Money that is owed.
2. d) Taking out a student loan to pay for postsecondary school.
3. a) Yes, because some kinds of debt are associated with appreciating assets.
4. b) Bad debt is money you owe associated with depreciating assets.
5. a) Good debt
6. b) When you borrow more money for college than you need.
7. b) Taking on student loans to obtain a higher education often results in your landing a better career, increasing your earning potential.
8. a) Good
9. d) All of these are bad debts.
10. a) If you do not, you will have to pay interest on top of what you owe.
11. c) Interest starts to accrue if your bill is not paid on time.
12. a) True
13. c) They count on the fact that many people will carry a balance on their card and thus make money from the interest.
14. d) Live simply in college, do not overspend, and do well in college so that the benefits of a college degree pay off for you later in life.
15. d) All answers are correct.

Too many adults spend too much of their hard-earned money on debt due to poor financial management. You will be the one to change the narrative of crushing debt by making more brilliant money moves from a young age.

It starts with being able to distinguish between good debts and bad ones. Once you know what kinds of debts to avoid, you can make wise money moves to ensure you stretch and maximize each dollar's power by following the simple and practical tips in this chapter.

I am sure you aced your quiz and are ready to tackle the next chapter. The flip side of the debt coin is, of course, credit. Understanding how credit works will help you level up your money game, making you a formidable contender on the financial scene filled with those who aim to wrangle your last hard-earned dollar with glitzy (empty) temptations and get-rich-quick schemes. Luckily, you will have learned, through this book and your own money-savvy smarts, to swipe left and give such pitfalls wrapped in opportunities and smacking of a good deal a wide berth.

11

BUILDING A POSITIVE CREDIT HISTORY

Before hitting her teen years, Bella Tipping had already established herself as a youngster in business. This is her story (Royale, 2020).

BELLA TIPPING: EMPOWERING KIDS IN TRAVEL WITH KIDZCATIONZ

At just 12 years old, Australian Bella Tipping had an extraordinary idea that would change the way families travel. Her family vacation left her feeling like the kids were often overlooked in favor of the adults. This experience ignited Bella's desire to create a solution, and Kidzcationz was born, a platform where children's voices matter.

Bella's parents, impressed by her determination, supported her vision. However, they insisted on a well-thought-out business plan before investing nearly $50,000. Bella treated them as serious investors, highlighting the importance of a solid plan to pursue one's dreams.

Kidzcationz stands out as it's entirely focused on providing children with a fun and educational travel experience. The platform uses avatars instead of real names and photos to ensure safety, creating a secure environment for kids to express themselves.

Bella's story is a beacon of inspiration for young entrepreneurs. It emphasizes that age should never be a hindrance to success. All it takes is a passion for change, a clear plan, and unwavering support from those who believe in your vision.

Kidzcationz is more than a website; it's a movement. It signifies the power of youth, innovation, and the belief that children's opinions are essential. Bella Tipping has given families a platform to ensure that every member, young or old, has a memorable and enriching travel experience. So, when you plan your next family vacation, remember Bella Tipping and Kidzcationz, and let your young explorers' voices be heard.

THE IMPORTANCE OF A GOOD CREDIT HISTORY

There are a few thoughts that teens should take more time to think about, like health insurance, taxes, social responsibility, and credit history! But it would be best if you started thinking about this important stuff now. Here are a few reasons why (Irby, 2023).

Financial Freedom Starts With Lower Interest Rates

Imagine a world where borrowing money doesn't cost an arm and a leg. With good credit, that world is within reach. Your credit score affects the interest rates you're offered. The higher your score, the lower your interest rates. This means less money going towards interest and more for the fun stuff in life.

Boost Your Confidence With Easier Approvals

Applying for a credit card or loan with a low credit score can be intimidating, but good credit changes the game. It doesn't guarantee approval, but it sure makes it more likely. It's like having an invisible cheerleader by your side, giving you the confidence to apply for what you want.

Flex Your Negotiating Power

Good credit gives you the upper hand when it comes to negotiating. It's like having a secret weapon. If you're unhappy with your current interest rates, a solid credit score empowers you to ask for a better deal. And having options to choose from means you're in control.

Unlock Higher Borrowing Limits

Who doesn't love flexibility when it comes to finances? Good credit opens the door to higher borrowing limits. Banks trust you more because you've shown you can manage your finances responsibly. This means bigger opportunities and more financial freedom.

Secure Your Dream Home

When it's time to leave the nest, your credit score can make a world of difference in finding your perfect place. Landlords often use credit scores to screen tenants. A good credit score ensures you'll have an easier time finding your dream apartment.

Drive Down Car Insurance Costs

Getting behind the wheel comes with expenses, and car insurance can be considerable. Insurers can consider your credit score when setting rates. Good credit can mean lower insurance premiums, so you can hit the road without emptying your pockets.

Say Goodbye to Security Deposits on Cellphones

Cellphone contracts are often elusive, with a low credit score. You might be stuck with pricey prepaid plans. But with good credit, you can say goodbye to security deposits and hello to the latest smartphones at discounted prices.

Skip Security Deposits on Utilities

Moving to a new place can be a hassle, and security deposits on utilities only add to the stress. A strong credit score ensures you won't have to pay these extra costs, making your move smoother and less expensive.

Bragging Rights of Responsible Money Management

Last but not least, good credit is something to be proud of. It's a testament to your financial responsibility and intelligent choices. Your friends may not have a clue about the benefits of good credit, but you can stand tall, knowing you're making your financial future brighter.

In conclusion, your credit score isn't just a number; it's a key that unlocks doors to financial freedom. So, start building good credit habits now, and you'll be well on your way to reaping the benefits in the future.

WHAT IS A CREDIT SCORE?

A credit score is a three-digit number, typically ranging from 300 to 850, that assesses your likelihood to repay borrowed money, such as credit card debt, car payments, and more. In the United States, three major credit bureaus—Equifax, TransUnion, and Experian—calculate credit scores using their own unique methods (*Everything Teens Should Know about Building Credit*, n.d.).

Credit Score Ranges:

Excellent credit: 800-850
Very good credit: 740-799
Good credit: 670-739
Fair credit: 580-669
Poor credit: 300-579 (Source: Equifax)

Factors That Determine Your Credit Score:

- **Payment History (35%):** Your payment history is a record of on-time and late payments on past loans and credit cards. It carries the most weight in determining your credit score. Late payments can lower your score, so always strive to pay your bills early or on time.
- **Amounts Owed (30%):** Also known as your debt-to-credit ratio, this factor indicates how much debt you owe compared to your available credit card limit. A general rule is to use no more than 30% of your available credit.
- **Length of Credit History (15%):** The length of your credit history matters. Your credit score is influenced by how long your credit accounts have been open, the age of your oldest and newest accounts, and the average age of all your accounts combined.

- **Types of Credit in Use (10%):** A variety of credit types, including auto loans, student loans, credit cards, and other lines of credit, can boost your credit score.
- **Account Inquiries (10%):** Each time you apply for credit (credit cards, loans, etc.), lenders review your credit score. Excessive inquiries can lower your score.

Where Can You Find Your Credit Score?

If you've never had credit cards, joint bank accounts, rental agreements, utility bills, or loans in your name, you might not yet have a credit score. For those with a credit history, you can obtain your credit report for free once a year at annualcreditreport.com. We recommend checking your credit score with a parent or guardian to ensure the security of your credit information.

How to Build Your Credit as a Teen:

- **Become an Authorized User:** If you have a trusted parent, guardian, or loved one, consider becoming an authorized user on their credit card account. This allows you to make purchases and begin building your credit. However, the primary account holder is ultimately responsible for payments, so ensure clear expectations about prompt payment. It is important that you choose a primary person with good credit. If they don't pay for their cards on time, this can lower your credit.
- **Apply for a Credit Card:** If becoming an authorized user isn't an option, and you're 18 or older, consider applying for a credit card. Given your limited or nonexistent credit history, you may qualify for a secured credit card, which requires an initial deposit (usually \$200-\$500) that becomes your credit limit. Timely payments on this card

help build a positive credit history, boosting your credit score and increasing your eligibility for larger credit amounts in the future. Explore alternative choices by checking if your bank or credit union provides student cashback cards or cards with low initial limits.

- **Joint Account:** A joint credit card allows two individuals to share an account, spend, update account details, and share equal responsibility for repayment. Applying for a joint account with a trusted person with a strong credit history can help you build your credit. However, be cautious, as you'll share the responsibility for any debt incurred on the card.

Tips to Avoid Damaging Your Credit:

- **Know the Basics:** Understanding the fundamentals of personal finance, such as the difference between checking and savings accounts, the fees for late payments, and what constitutes a good credit score, is crucial.
- **Pay Your Bills on Time:** One late payment can negatively impact your credit score, so always strive to pay your bills within 30 days or less. Setting up automatic payments for at least the minimum is advisable to avoid a costly mistake.
- **Keep Credit Card Balances Low:** Aim to keep your credit card balances well below your available credit limit. Your credit utilization ratio plays a role in determining your credit score.
- **Stick to One Credit Card:** Applying for multiple credit cards too quickly can lower your credit score and signal to lenders that you may not be responsible with money.

Building your credit takes time and effort, but it's a crucial part of securing your financial future. If you have questions about credit or finance, consider discussing them with a trusted adult.

ACTIVITY: CREDIT SCORE QUIZ

How Much Do You Know About Your Credit Scores? Take Our Quiz and Find Out (*Quiz: How Much Do You Know about Credit Scores? | Equifax®*, n.d.)!

1. Which of the following factors can influence your credit scores?

A) Your favorite color
B) The number of pets you have
C) Your payment history
D) The weather in your area

2. What does a good payment history mean for your credit scores?

A) It doesn't have any impact.
B) It can improve your credit scores.
C) It can lower your credit scores.
D) It only affects your credit reports.

3. How often are you entitled to a free copy of your credit reports from each of the three nationwide credit bureaus?

A) Every three months
B) Every six months
C) Once a year
D) Only when you apply for a loan

4. What does "credit utilization" refer to?

A) How many credit cards do you own
B) The ratio of credit you're using compared to the total amount available to you
C) The total amount of credit you've ever had
D) The type of credit accounts you have

5. Which of the following factors is generally the most significant in determining your credit scores?

A) The length of your credit history
B) The number of times you've applied for credit recently
C) The types of credit accounts you have
D) Your payment history

6. Can your credit scores change over time?

A) No, they stay the same once calculated.
B) Yes, they can change based on your financial behaviors.
C) Only when you apply for new credit.
D) Only if you have a high income.

7. What is a credit score used for?

A) To determine your favorite TV shows
B) To predict the weather
C) To assess your credit risk and likelihood of paying bills on time
D) To recommend restaurants in your area

8. How many credit bureaus are there that compile and maintain credit reports?

A) One
B) Two
C) Three
D) Five

9. What does a "soft inquiry" on your credit report usually indicate?

A) A routine credit check by a lender
B) A potential employer checking your credit
C) Your own request for a copy of your credit report
D) A late payment on a bill

10. How long does negative information, like late payments, typically stay on your credit report?

A) 30 days
B) 6 months
C) 2 years
D) 7-10 years

Answers:

1. C. Your payment history.
2. B. It can improve your credit scores.
3. C. Once a year.
4. B. The ratio of credit you're using compared to the total amount available to you.
5. D. Your payment history.
6. B. Yes, they can change based on your financial behaviors.

7. C. To assess your credit risk and likelihood of paying bills on time.
8. C. Three.
9. C. Your own request for a copy of your credit report.
10. D. 7–10 years.

How did you do? Understanding your credit scores is essential for managing your financial health and making informed decisions. If you have any questions or want to learn more about credit scores, feel free to explore reliable resources and consult with financial experts.

Starting on your financial journey can be as exciting and fulfilling or as scary and overwhelming as you choose for it to be. The key, of course, is to learn as much as possible and embark on this lifelong voyage with your eyes open.

On the subject of learning, the next chapter deals with how to level up your earning power by acquiring the right skill set through higher education. Mapping the trajectory of your career is something you don't want to downplay. Smart, motivated, and money-savvy teens understand that, as with most things, you have to put in the effort to see tangible results.

PART V

STEPPING STONES TO SUCCESS: EDUCATION AND CAREER PATH

12

PLANNING YOUR CAREER AND HIGHER EDUCATION

Kamaria Warren is a young entrepreneur who has turned her passion into a thriving business (Lodge, 2019). Her story is both inspiring and impactful. At just seven years old, Kamaria embarked on a journey that would shape her future and inspire countless others.

While searching for birthday invitations, she noticed a lack of products representing girls like her, such as brown and black. Instead of accepting the situation, Kamaria saw an opportunity. With the support of her mom, graphic designer Shaunice Sasser, Kamaria founded Brown Girls Stationery. This brand celebrates diversity and empowerment.

Kamaria's business offers a range of products, including party and school supplies, stationery, vegan purses, and accessories, each featuring cheerful illustrations of black and brown girls. In addition to her creative offerings, Kamaria also sells dolls, spreading a message of inclusivity and representation.

Despite her young age, Kamaria's business has flourished. She operates her enterprise with a team of dedicated employees and volunteers, making a difference in girls' lives everywhere. Through platforms like Shopify, Faire Marketplace, and local events, Kamaria has sold thousands of notebooks, notepads, and backpacks yearly. And she doesn't stop there; she continues to expand her product line, introducing new items like party supplies, lip glosses, and purses, each designed to empower and inspire.

Kamaria's motivation goes beyond financial success. The real reward for her is seeing other girls proudly wear her creations and embrace their unique identities. Her motto, "Dear Brown girl, you can change the world," resonates with her products and spirit.

Kamaria's story teaches us a valuable lesson: failure and fear should never hinder your entrepreneurial journey. Instead, view setbacks as opportunities to learn and grow, refine your strategies, and move forward with newfound determination.

Kamaria Warren's journey reminds us that age is no barrier to success; your passion and determination can change the world.

WHAT YOU SHOULD KNOW

The temptation to forgo a tertiary education in the face of a meager start-up income is a trap that too many high school graduates fall into; most of the time, due to family finances, full-time Higher education is not an option (Torpey, 2015).

Discover Your Passion

As you navigate through high school, it's the perfect time to embark on a journey of self-discovery. High school years fly by, and it's important to start exploring your interests and passions early. Discovering your passion can lay the foundation for a fulfilling future.

High school isn't just about books and exams; it's a place to identify what truly excites you. Your interests may evolve and change over time, so stay open to new experiences and ideas.

Connect Interests to Careers

Once you have a better sense of your passion, it's time to connect the dots between your interests and potential careers. Exploring careers that align with your passions is like choosing your adventure in the world of work.

You don't need to have it all figured out now. Still, you're setting yourself up for success by exploring various career paths related to your interests. Speak with mentors and teachers, and use online resources to uncover career options that match your passions.

Get Real-World Insights

Discovering your dream career goes beyond just reading about it in books or on websites. To truly understand what a job entails, you should gather real-world insights. It's like trying on a pair of shoes before buying them.

Consider informational interviews and job shadowing experiences. This is an opportunity to chat with professionals who work in your dream job and even spend a day in their shoes. It's like getting a sneak peek behind the scenes; it can be eye-opening.

Learn by Doing

High school is the perfect time to gain hands-on experience. Think of it as dipping your toes into the pool before diving in. Internships, part-time jobs, and volunteering can give you a taste of what it's like in the real world.

These experiences are more than just a line on your resume. They help you figure out what you enjoy and what you might want to steer clear of. You'll also develop crucial skills like teamwork, time management, and communication that'll benefit you in any career.

Plan Your Path

Success in your dream career requires a solid plan. Think of it like plotting a course on a map before embarking on an exciting journey. Start considering the education and training you'll need.

High school can be a launch pad for your future. Look into advanced classes and programs that will prepare you for the path ahead. Your high school counselor can be your trusty guide, helping you choose the right courses and chart your educational pathway.

Tailor Your Training

Every career is unique, just like you are. Training is the key to unlocking the door to your dream job. Whether it's hands-on experience, apprenticeships, certificates, or degrees, the path to your dream career is yours to tailor.

Imagine it like a wardrobe with various outfits to choose from. Some careers require a short apprenticeship, while others demand a longer educational journey. High school can prepare you for this adventure by guiding you to the right tailor.

Prepare for College Adventures

College can be like stepping into a new world with endless possibilities. To make the most of this adventure, you should prepare yourself. It's like packing your bags with all the essentials for a grand journey.

High school can provide the stepping stones you need to make a smooth transition into college. Enroll in courses that match your career goals and consider advanced programs. Think of it as gaining exceptional skills and tools for your upcoming adventure.

Flexibility and Chasing Dreams

Remember, your career journey is not set in stone. You're more like a sailor on the sea of life, free to change course. Sometimes, you might choose a different route, and that's perfectly fine.

Be open to changes because life's full of surprises. You can even take a "gap year" after high school to explore your passions or gain new experiences. Think of it as a detour that might lead to your true path.

Seek Guidance and Stay Curious

You don't have to go through this adventure alone. Seek advice from mentors, teachers, and those who've embarked on similar journeys. They can be your trusty companions, guiding you along the way.

Explore different paths, keep asking questions, and stay curious. Your journey to a dream career is a dynamic adventure of self-discovery, exploration, and continuous growth. Remember that the world is full of opportunities, and your unique path awaits your exploration.

NAVIGATING THE WORLD OF COLLEGE FINANCE: FINANCIAL AID AND STUDENT LOANS

So, you're on the brink of one of the most exciting adventures of your life, college! But the looming question remains, "*How do I pay for it?*" The answer is simpler than you think. Let's dive into the world of financial aid and student loans and discover the options that will make your dream education a reality (*Financial Aid for Students | USAGov*, n.d.).

Free Application for Federal Student Aid (FAFSA)

The first stop on your college finance journey is the Free Application for Federal Student Aid, or FAFSA for short. This is your golden ticket to unlocking a world of financial support, including grants, loans, work-study programs, and more. Applying for FAFSA is as crucial as packing your favorite snacks for the dorm.

Types of Student Financial Aid

When financing your education, the toolbox is filled with various tools. You've got grants, like gifts you don't have to repay. Scholarships are like winning the lottery but with your academic prowess. Then there are work-study programs, where you can earn while you learn. Lastly, loans can provide a helping hand today but come with the responsibility of repayment tomorrow.

Before you start daydreaming about your college experience, it's essential to have a clear understanding of the costs. Online tools and calculators can help you estimate how much your dream college will set you back. This knowledge will empower you to make informed decisions and find the perfect fit for your budget.

Get Started Repaying Your Federal Student Loan

Yes, it's a bit early to think about repaying your student loans, but hey, preparation is key! Your journey to becoming financially responsible starts here. Make a plan for loan repayment before the due date approaches. Learn how to manage payments so you're not drowning in debt after graduation.

Resolve Student Loan Payment Problems

Life happens, and sometimes, loan payments can feel overwhelming. Don't hide your head in the sand if you struggle to make payments. Contact your loan servicer because ignoring your student loan has serious consequences. Together, you can find a solution that brightens your financial future.

FAFSA in Detail

FAFSA is your passport for financial aid, but what are the nitty-gritty details?

1. **Federal Deadlines:** You must meet deadlines to be considered for federal student aid. The next one is on June 30, 2024, for the 2023-24 school year. Mark it on your calendar!

2. **Creating an FSA ID:** It's like your secret code to access federal aid. Get an FSA ID, username, and password combination to smooth your FAFSA journey.
3. **Fill out the FAFSA:** You'll need various information to complete the FAFSA. Gather them all so you're well-prepared.
4. **Eligibility for Federal Aid:** Certain eligibility criteria must be met. Financial need is often a factor, but make sure you qualify before proceeding.
5. **Check Your FAFSA Application Status:** After you've submitted your FAFSA, stay in the loop by checking your application status. You can do this by logging in to your account or contacting the Federal Student Aid Information Center.

Choosing the Right College

Picking the perfect college is like finding the right pair of shoes; it has to fit just right. Start by understanding what's included in the total cost of college. Look at the costs for the specific schools you're considering. Pay attention to other expenses, ways to cut costs, and how to compare the financial aspects of different colleges.

Tools to Help You Find the Perfect Fit

The Department of Education offers some handy tools to make your college search a breeze:

1. **College Navigator:** Use it to find schools that match your academic and financial needs.
2. **College Scorecard:** Compare schools based on price, field of study, and other criteria.

3. **Net Price Calculator Center:** Estimate the cost of attending a specific school, factoring in scholarships and grants.

Repaying Student Loans

Even though repaying your student loans might seem light years away, the process starts sooner than you think. Interest on student loans restarts on September 1, so be prepared for payments to resume in October. Make a repayment plan and understand the different repayment options available to you.

Student Loan Forgiveness

If you're considering a career in public service or education, there are loan forgiveness programs tailored for you:

- **Public Service Loan Forgiveness:** This program may be your ticket to loan forgiveness if you work for a U.S. government or not-for-profit organization.
- **Teacher Loan Forgiveness:** If you're a full-time teacher in a low-income school or educational service agency for five consecutive years, you may qualify.
- **Healthcare Loan Forgiveness:** Medical researchers and clinicians working in specific healthcare programs can also benefit from loan forgiveness.

Dealing With Loan Payment Problems

Should you ever find yourself struggling to repay your student loans, don't panic. You can explore options like loan deferment or forbearance, which offer temporary relief from payments. But remember, delinquency and default have severe consequences, so it's essential to keep the lines of communication open with your loan servicer.

Now that you have a bird's eye view of the financial aid and student loan landscape, you're well-equipped to start your college journey. Remember, it's all about making informed decisions and setting yourself up for a bright and financially secure future. Good luck, future scholars!

In our pursuit of wealth, we often risk getting side-tracked by the gleam of immediate wealth. As a result, the prospect of spending four-plus years of your life studying, starving, and stressing to end up with student loan repayments and no job can be challenging. However, you are smart enough to understand that good things come to those who wait. In that case, you will understand how important getting a degree or diploma is to realizing your long-term financial goals. There are loads of financial aid options you can look into and loads of colleges that can help you unlock your earning potential.

Congratulations on making the most important life decision, starting your journey to financial security from a tender age. You understand that life is about balance, priorities, and striving for higher goals and a better future, one that is filled with endless possibilities, opportunities, and accomplishments.

Be the Inspiration!

You have a bright and abundant future ahead of you, and you have all the tools you need to make sure you reach it … that puts you in an excellent position to inspire someone else!

Simply by sharing your honest opinion of this book and a little about what you've discovered, you'll help other teenagers get started on their own empowering journey into a successful future.

Thank you so much for your support. Now, get out there and seize the day!

Scan the QR code below

CONCLUSION

As we wrap up this journey through the world of personal finance for teens, let's revisit the main message of this book: This guide equips teenagers and young adults with essential knowledge and practical skills to make informed financial decisions, setting you on a path of lifelong financial success.

Throughout this book, we've explored the fundamentals of financial literacy, from understanding the importance of budgeting, saving, and investing to mastering the art of making informed financial decisions. We've demystified concepts like compound interest, diversified portfolios, and the magic of long-term investing. But more than just financial jargon, we've delved into the practical steps and strategies that will empower you to take control of your financial future.

In the world of personal finance, there's a key takeaway that we want to reinforce and bring home: Financial literacy and early investing are the keys to building lasting wealth. It's a simple yet profound truth that bears repeating. It's not about how much money you have right now; it's about what you do with it and how you grow it over time. Your financial journey is a marathon, not a sprint; the earlier you start, the better off you'll be.

Now, let's end on a high note with an inspiring success story, a tale of determination, innovation, and youthful ambition that serves as a testament to the extraordinary possibilities within your reach.

BRIAN WONG: TURNING DREAMS INTO REALITY

Brian Wong's story is nothing short of remarkable (Royale, 2020). Unlike some of the teenage entrepreneurs you've encountered in this book, Brian was a success at school. In fact, he was an academic prodigy. He graduated high school at 14, a feat that already set him apart from his peers.

By 18, Brian had earned his university degree. While many teenagers were still figuring out their career paths, Brian was already charting his own. He recognized that he had the potential to achieve something extraordinary, and he was determined to do just that.

While at university, Brian launched his first company, a venture that would foreshadow his future success. His company aimed to help users find the best Twitter feeds to follow based on their interests, showcasing his early entrepreneurial spirit and knack for identifying market needs.

However, his next venture truly propelled him into the spotlight. At the age of 19, Brian conceived an idea that would revolutionize the world of mobile gaming and, in the process, earn him a spot among the most influential young entrepreneurs of his time. He co-founded Kiip, a groundbreaking concept that allowed real-world rewards to be attached to success in mobile games.

The concept was ingenious. Players could unlock tangible, real-world prizes instead of merely earning virtual rewards for in-game accomplishments. For instance, achieving a high score might reward players with discount codes for their favorite shops, free movie tickets, or even a free meal at a popular restaurant. It was a game-changer, pun intended.

The beauty of Kiip lay in its simplicity and the way it tapped into our natural desire for rewards. Gamification had taken on a new dimension, and advertisers recognized the potential of this innovative platform to engage and connect with a vast audience.

One of Brian's boldest moves was securing venture capital funding for Kiip. At an age when most young adults are still figuring out their majors in college, Brian was pitching his entrepreneurial vision to investors. And he succeeded. He secured the support he needed to develop Kiip and take it to the next level.

Today, Kiip is a household name in the tech industry, used by over 400 apps on a staggering 300 million devices worldwide. Brian Wong's visionary approach to mobile advertising not only brought financial success but also made him a shining example of what a determined young entrepreneur can achieve.

YOUR PATH TO LIFELONG FINANCIAL SUCCESS

Brian Wong's journey is a testament to what's possible when passion, dedication, and a willingness to take risks converge. His story underlines the idea that age is no barrier to achieving extraordinary success. It also illustrates how entrepreneurship and innovation can create opportunities and transform industries.

But what does this mean for you, our young readers? It means your dreams are valid, and your aspirations can be realized. You have the tools and resources at your disposal to create a bright financial future, just like Brian did.

Throughout this book, we've covered the essential building blocks of personal finance. You've acquired a solid foundation from understanding the power of compounding and the importance of budgeting to demystifying investment strategies and managing debt. You now have the knowledge and skills to make informed financial decisions, navigate the complex world of money, and lay the groundwork for a prosperous future.

KEY TAKEAWAYS

As you close this chapter and step into your own journey, remember the following key takeaways:

1. **Financial Literacy Matters:** The more you understand money, the better equipped you are to make smart financial decisions. Take the time to continue your financial education through books, online courses, or conversations with experts. Never stop learning.
2. **Start Early:** Brian Wong's story echoes this point. The earlier you start saving and investing, even if you have very little money, the more time you'll have to let your money grow. Compound interest is your greatest ally. Don't underestimate the power of time in building wealth.
3. **Budgeting Is Your Foundation:** A well-structured budget is the cornerstone of your financial success. It keeps your spending in check, ensures you save consistently, and helps you allocate money for investments. Make budgeting a habit, and you'll have control over your financial destiny.
4. **Diversify Your Portfolio:** When you begin investing, diversify your portfolio to spread risk. Invest in a mix of

assets like stocks, bonds, and real estate. This diversification strategy helps protect your investments from market fluctuations.

5. **Stay Debt-Aware:** Not all debt is bad, but it's essential to manage it wisely. High-interest debts like credit card debt can erode your wealth, while low-interest debts, like mortgages, can help you build assets. Be mindful of your debt and make strategic decisions.
6. **Emergency Funds Are Lifesavers:** Life is unpredictable, and unexpected expenses can throw a wrench in your financial plans. An emergency fund provides a financial safety net, so you're prepared for the unexpected.
7. **Seek Advice and Support:** Don't hesitate to seek guidance from financial advisors, mentors, and family members. A supportive network can provide valuable insights and encouragement on your financial journey.
8. **Start making wise money decisions today for a prosperous future:** The knowledge you've gained from this book is your toolbox. Put it to work, and take that first step towards financial security. Set your financial goals and work diligently towards achieving them.

Unlock the doors to financial independence by investing today, even with little money. As you've learned from the stories and advice in this book, the journey to financial freedom begins with that first investment. It's not about the amount; it's about getting started. Invest consistently, stay patient, and watch your wealth grow.

But before we part ways, I have one last request. If you found this book helpful or inspirational, please leave a review. Your feedback can inspire and guide other teens on their journey to financial success.

Thank you for taking this important step toward securing your financial future. As you move forward, remember that the future is bright, and your financial success is within reach. The world is full of opportunities, just waiting for ambitious young individuals like you to seize them. So go out there and make your dreams a reality. You've got this!

REFERENCES

6 Secrets to becoming an inspiring teen leader! (2023). We Think Twice. https://www.wethinktwice.acf.hhs.gov/6-secrets-becoming-inspiring-teen-leader

7 Reasons You Need to Set Financial Goals. (2017, September 5). Money Nuggets. https://www.moneynuggets.co.uk/important-to-set-financial-goals/

10 Strategies to avoid getting into debt | central bank. (n.d.). Www.centralbank.net. https://www.centralbank.net/learning-center/strategies-to-avoid-debt/

Abella, A. (2023, August 31). *Robo-Advisors and young investors.* Investopedia. https://www.investopedia.com/articles/investing/121615/are-roboadvisors-good-idea-young-investors.asp

Alexandra Twin. (2021, December 17). *Refinance: How and when it happens.* Investopedia. https://www.investopedia.com/terms/r/refinance.asp

Bennett, R. (2023, June 7). *How to choose a bank: 8 steps to take.* Bankrate. https://www.bankrate.com/banking/how-to-choose-a-bank/#s5

Benve, R. (2023, July 20). How to set SMART personal financial goals. *ToughNickel.* https://toughnickel.com/personal-finance/How-to-Set-Personal-Financial-Goals-Budgeting

CEPF, L. G. T. (n.d.). *There are 6 types of saving accounts, and the best option for you depends on how and when you want to access your money.* Business Insider. https://www.businessinsider.com/personal-finance/types-of-savings-accounts

Cherry, K. (2019). *17 Ways to develop your creativity.* Verywell Mind. https://www.verywellmind.com/how-to-boost-your-creativity-2795046

Colestock, S. (2023, February 27). *Best money and budgeting apps for kids, teens and young adults.* The Dough Roller. https://www.doughroller.net/personal-finance/budgeting/best-money-apps-for-kids-teens-and-young-adults/

Compound interest calculator | investor.gov. (n.d.). Www.investor.gov. https://www.investor.gov/financial-tools-calculators/calculators/compound-interest-calculator

Costill, A. (2016, December 9). *25 Kids that made $1 million before graduating high school.* Due. https://due.com/25-kids-made-1-million-graduating-high-school/

Crevin, M. (2020, July 14). *Listen more, talk less and other tips for better communication - your teen mag.* Your Teen Magazine. https://yourteenmag.com/family-life/communication/ways-to-improve-communication

Cueto, C. (2022, December 30). *9 steps to developing a positive money mindset.* Prosper. https://www.prosper.com/blog/better-money-habits-positive-money-mindset

Davis, C. (n.d.). *Fractional shares: What they are and where to buy them.* NerdWallet. https://www.nerdwallet.com/article/investing/fractional-shares

Empowering teen entrepreneurs: A comprehensive guide - Crimson Education ZA. (2023, June 15). Www.crimsoneducation.org. https://www.crimsoneducation.org/za/blog/high-school-entrepreneurship/

Everything teens should know about building credit. (n.d.). Getschooled.com. https://getschooled.com/article/5787-teens-and-credit-scores/

Fernando, J. (2023, March 28). *Time value of money (TVM).* Investopedia. https://www.investopedia.com/terms/t/timevalueofmoney.asp

Field, H. (2021, December 8). *These two examples illustrate the magic of compound interest.* HerMoney. https://hermoney.com/invest/retirement/these-two-examples-illustrate-the-magic-of-compound-interest/

Financial aid for students | USAGov. (n.d.). Www.usa.gov. https://www.usa.gov/financial-aid

Financial, S. (2018, February 21). *Understanding the four pillars of personal finance.* Spero Financial. https://spero.financial/understanding-the-four-pillars-of-personal-finance/

FRANKENFIELD, J. (2018). *Checking account.* Investopedia. https://www.investopedia.com/terms/c/checkingaccount.asp

Geier, B. (2021, February 10). *10 Types of investments (and how they work).* SmartAsset. https://smartasset.com/investing/types-of-investment

George, D. (2021). *6 Advantages and 4 disadvantages of online banking.* Nasdaq.com. https://www.nasdaq.com/articles/6-advantages-and-4-disadvantages-of-online-banking

Grable, J. E., & Lytton, R. H. (2020). *Online survey software | Qualtrics Survey Solutions.* Qualtrics.com. https://missouri.qualtrics.com/jfe/form/SV_e5O9zdPbe1NDMWh

Hackett, F. (2023, February 6). *Tips for teens: How to find your first real job.* ResumeBuilder.com. https://www.resumebuilder.com/tips-for-teens-how-to-find-your-first-real-job/

Hill, Andy. *200 Empowering Quotes About Money and Personal Finance.* Marriage Kids and Money. Last modified June 29, 2017. https://marriagekidsandmoney.com/20-empowering-quotes-about-money-and-personal-finance/

How to Become a Teenage Millionaire: 15 Success Stories. (2018, September 28). *How to become a teenage millionaire: 15 success stories | ProfileTree.* Profiletree.com. https://profiletree.com/teenage-millionaire/

How to open a bank account as a teen. (n.d.). Getschooled.com. Retrieved October 15,

2023, from https://getschooled.com/article/5967-how-to-open-a-bank-account-as-a-teen/

Irby, L. (2023, January 5). *9 Benefits of having a good credit score.* The Balance. https://www.thebalancemoney.com/having-good-credit-score-960528

Kagan, J. (2019). *Retirement planning.* Investopedia. https://www.investopedia.com/terms/r/retirement-planning.asp

Kagan, J. (2020, May 11). *Peer-to-Peer lending: The lowdown.* Investopedia. https://www.investopedia.com/terms/p/peer-to-peer-lending.asp

Kaspersky. (2022). *What is cryptocurrency and how does it work?* Kaspersky. https://www.kaspersky.com/resource-center/definitions/what-is-cryptocurrency

Kunze, J. (2016). *Good debt vs. bad debt | 404 plays | Quizizz.* Quizizz.com. https://quizizz.com/admin/quiz/58ed619459c4f4632d08d1ba/good-debt-vs-bad-debt

Leavitt, L. (2023, August 29). *Rule of 72: What it is and how to use it.* Bankrate. https://www.bankrate.com/investing/what-is-the-rule-of-72/

Lee, A. (2021, September 21). *How to teach needs vs wants for kids & teens.* Mydoh. https://www.mydoh.ca/learn/blog/education/how-to-teach-kids-teens-the-difference-between-needs-vs-wants/

Lodge, M. (2019, October 25). 10 Successful young entrepreneurs. *Investopedia.* https://www.investopedia.com/10-successful-young-entrepreneurs-4773310

Mint. (2022, June 30). *Budgeting for teens: 14 tips for growing your money young.* MintLife Blog. https://mint.intuit.com/blog/budgeting/budgeting-for-teens/

Modu, E. (2023, July 21). *Index funds for teen investors (and kids).* TeenVestor. https://www.teenvestor.com/index-funds-for-teen-investors

Mom, R. C. (2023, February 23). *10 College application tips to make your teen's life easier.* Rocket City Mom | Huntsville Events, Activities, and Resources for Families. https://www.rocketcitymom.com/blog/2023/02/23/10-college-application-tips-to-make-your-teens-life-easier/#:~:text=Start%20by%20researching%20the%20schools

Mydoh. (2023, May 3). *Emergency funds explained for teens.* Mydoh. https://www.mydoh.ca/learn/money-101/building-credit/emergency-funds-explained-for-teens/

Now is the most important time to focus on teen mental health. (2021, July). Www.discovery.co.za. https://www.discovery.co.za/corporate/health-teen-mental-health

O Niell, S. (2023, June 23). *Understanding risk and reward - meet Sean O'Neill.* Meet Sean 'O Niell. https://meetseanoneill.com/understanding-risk-and-reward/

O'Shea, A. (2021, August 18). *Types of investments.* NerdWallet. https://www.nerdwallet.com/article/investing/types-of-investments

Patterson, T. (2020, February 18). *Top 5 ways to protect your bank accounts.* SmartAsset. https://smartasset.com/checking-account/top-5-ways-to-protect-your-bank-accounts

Personal finance quiz & financial literacy questions. (n.d.). Council for Economic Education. Retrieved October 17, 2023, from https://www.councilforeconed.org/personal-finance-quiz/

Puharich, R. (2021, October 17). *13 Reasons to save money as a teenager - Teenlearner.* TeenLearner. https://teenlearner.com/13-reasons-to-save-money-as-a-teenager/

Puharich, R. (2022, February 17). *How to start a business as a teenager with no money - TeenLearner.* Teen Learner. https://teenlearner.com/start-a-business-as-a-teenager-with-no-money/

Pyles, S. (n.d.). *Good debt vs. bad debt: Examples and solutions.* NerdWallet. https://www.nerdwallet.com/article/finance/good-debt-vs-bad-debt

Quiz: How much do you know about credit scores? | Equifax®. (n.d.). Www.equifax.com. Retrieved November 5, 2023, from https://www.equifax.com/personal/education/credit/score/articles/-/learn/credit-score-quiz/

Raising Children Network. (2019, February 5). *Pre-teen and teenage mental health.* Raising Children Network. https://raisingchildren.net.au/pre-teens/mental-health-physical-health/about-mental-health/teen-mental-health

Royale, O. (2020, October 20). *14 Teen entrepreneurs and how they succeeded.* Oxford Royale Academy. https://www.oxford-royale.com/articles/14-teen-entrepreneurs/

Sabrina. (2020). *9 Powerful benefits of setting financial goals - finance over fifty.* Finance over Fifty. https://financeoverfifty.com/benefits-of-setting-financial-goals/

Segal, T. (n.d.). *What Is a Custodial Account?* Investopedia. https://www.investopedia.com/terms/c/custodialaccount.asp

Setting a SMART savings goal SAVINGS CHECKING Accounts. (n.d.). Retrieved October 8, 2023, from https://fhi360.org/sites/default/files/media/documents/cfpb_building_block_activities_setting-smart-savings-goal_worksheet.pdf

Shank, S. (2015, May 18). *10 reasons why teens should start a business.* Encouraging Moms at Home. https://encouragingmomsathome.com/10-reasons-teens-start-business/

Short, medium and long term financial goals (video). (n.d.). Khan Academy. Retrieved October 1, 2023, from https://www.khanacademy.org/college-careers-more/financial-literacy/xa6995ea67a8e9fdd:financial-goals/xa6995ea67a8e9fdd:short-medium-and-long-term-goals/v/short-medium-and-long-term-financial-goals

Souers, M. (2022, January 21). *Public speaking: Getting beyond the fear through the three P's*. Blogs.ifas.ufl.edu. https://blogs.ifas.ufl.edu/orangeco/2022/01/21/public-speaking-getting-beyond-the-fear-through-the-three-ps/

Squad, T. S. (2021a, September 20). *5 Teen entrepreneurs whose success stories wow and inspire*. The Startup Squad. https://www.thestartupsquad.com/5-teen-entrepreneurs-whose-success-stories-wow-and-inspire/

Squad, T. S. (2021b, September 20). *5 Teen entrepreneurs whose success stories wow and inspire.* The Startup Squad. https://www.thestartupsquad.com/5-teen-entrepreneurs-whose-success-stories-wow-and-inspire/

Srivastav, A. K. (2018, May 28). *Annuity vs perpetuity*. WallStreetMojo. https://www.wallstreetmojo.com/annuity-vs-perpetuity/

Staff, C. R. (n.d.). *Creating a final choice college checklist - college raptor*. College Raptor Blog. Retrieved November 7, 2023, from https://www.collegeraptor.com/find-colleges/articles/college-search/creating-a-final-choice-college-checklist/

Teen investors exchange-traded funds. (n.d.). TeenVestor. https://www.teenvestor.com/teen-investors-etf

Test your risk tolerance - BCSC investright. (2016, August 8). Investright. https://www.investright.org/manage-investments/key-concepts/test-your-risk-tolerance/

The calculator site. (2019). *Compound interest calculator - the calculator site*. The Calculator Site; Compound Int. https://www.thecalculatorsite.com/finance/calculators/compoundinterestcalculator.php

The teen millionaires making their own fortune. (2020, March 6). Lovemoney.com. https://www.lovemoney.com/galleries/65023/the-teen-millionaires-making-their-own-fortune?page=2

Tim. (2020, October 26). *3 Steps to align your money with your values*. Atypical Finance. https://www.atypicalfinance.com/3-steps-to-align-your-money-with-your-values/

Torpey, E. (2015, January 7). *Career planning for high schoolers : Career outlook: U.S. Bureau of Labor Statistics*. Bls.gov. https://www.bls.gov/careeroutlook/2015/article/career-planning-for-high-schoolers.htm

Turner, T. (2023, February 3). *47+ Fascinating financial literacy statistics in 2022.* Annuity.org. https://www.annuity.org/financial-literacy/financial-literacy-statistics/

Ultimate guide: How to earn money as a teenager. (n.d.). Www.getcopper.com. https://www.getcopper.com/guide/earning

VanSomeren, K. (n.d.). *Keep your budget simple with the 50/30/20 rule*. The Balance. https://www.thebalancemoney.com/the-50-30-20-rule-of-thumb-453922

Wall Strategies. (2020). *Delayed gratification and money success* - Wallstrategies.com. https://wallstrategies.com/delayed-gratification-and-money-success/

What is compound growth - Wells Fargo. (n.d.). Www.wellsfargo.com. https://www.wellsfargo.com/financial-education/investing/compound-interest-growth/
Why teens should open a bank account. (n.d.). Getschooled.com. Retrieved October 15, 2023, from https://getschooled.com/article/5966-why-teens-should-open-a-bank-account/

Made in United States
Cleveland, OH
04 November 2026

47645125R00126